BEST POI

THE BOOK OF FIVE MARKINGS

IVOR GURNEY

BEST POEMS and
THE BOOK OF FIVE MAKINGS

EDITED BY
R.K.R. THORNTON
&
GEORGE WALTER

Mid Northumberland Arts Group

Carcanet Press

First published in 1995 by
Mid Northumberland Arts Group
Wansbeck Square
Ashington
Northumberland NE63 9XL

in association with

Carcanet Press Limited
402–406 Corn Exchange Buildings
Manchester M4 3BY

A CIP catalogue record for this book
is available from the British Library
ISBN 0 904790 87 8 (MidNAG)
ISBN 1 85754 200 2 (Carcanet)

The publishers acknowledge financial assistance
from the Arts Council of England and Northern Arts

Set in 10½/12pt Ehrhardt by XL Publishing Services, Nairn
Printed and bound in England by SRP Ltd, Exeter

Contents

Introduction

Ivor Gurney has begun to achieve the recognition that he always felt was his due. He has been the subject of a well-received biography; he has had his poems published in an acclaimed collected edition; he has had his letters collected and published; he has had many volumes of his song settings published; he has been the subject of articles in journals and of academic doctoral dissertations both in England and the United States; his poetry has been widely represented in anthologies; a bibliography has been prepared and a revision of it will be published this year; his music has been frequently broadcast and recorded; he has had concerts devoted to his work; he has even been the special subject of a contestant in *Mastermind*; and he now has a society dedicated to the promotion of interest in his work.

Yet this recognition has some omissions. The *Collected Letters* stopped at 1922 when Gurney went into the City of London Mental Hospital at Dartford. The *Collected Poems* were, as P.J. Kavanagh wrote in his 'Editorial Note', 'not a "complete Gurney", even less a complete variant edition'; and he added quite reasonably that 'It would hardly be possible, and certainly unfair to Gurney, to print everything he wrote.' The music has been examined by several musicians and the conclusion has been justly drawn that, although there are still some pieces which yet deserve to be heard, not all of it is worth publishing. The combined effect of all this is twofold: first it means that Gurney has not been presented to the public in the way in which most poets find their audience, and second it means that the asylum period has come to seem almost as a dark abyss of disintegration into which Gurney goes towards destruction. Our Chronology lays emphasis on the later period to indicate something of the activity of the asylum years.

Ivor Gurney's career as a poet was unlike that of most other writers. He did not have a steady publication of small books of poems, later to be collected in large editions and selections. He began in 1917 and 1919 with two small books of poems, *Severn & Somme* and *War's Embers*, and then in 1922 entered the asylum from which only a little music and an occasional poem in magazines emerged. But he did not stop writing, and he did not stop writing impressively or indeed developing. He produced innumerable pages of poetic material (as well as much music) from which Edmund Blunden (1954), Leonard Clark (1973) and finally and most importantly P.J. Kavanagh (1982) have produced impressive selected and *Collected Poems*. He thus went from the small editions to the 'Collected' in one immense leap, a process which obscures to some extent his growth and development, and disguises how he kept writing well into the asylum period.

It is worth reinventing the conventional process and considering what Gurney might have published, what he would have assembled to represent himself. In fact he did put collections together, just as John Clare did in the early 1830s. When there seemed little hope of publication, Clare collected in *The Midsummer Cushion* his poems of the late 1820s and early 1830s and copied them into a ledger complete with title page, dedication and introduction; it was not published until 1979. So Gurney in the 1920s collected poems together in exercise books, and in groups, and was interested in having them published. More than that, he pleaded to have his work published, feeling that it had undeniable merit. We know some of the titles: *Rewards of Wonder* (whose complex history George Walter has unravelled), *Eighty Poems*, *The book of Five makings*, and *Best poems*. These all work towards a statement of his poetic position, and come from his viewpoint and not from the viewpoint of a selector or editor. It is important to see his work from this perspective.

As an example of his industry and exasperation, look at a document (GA 52.11.137) of the mid 1920s, perhaps August 1924, where Gurney asks in despair 'Why don't you – some of you – settle things? My war books alone have magnificent things. The war music too.' He lists books which he wishes to read (Skelton, Kipling in French, Dolben, Meredith, Drummond of Hawthornden, Blunden, Clare, Sassoon, Hardy, Plutarch, Wilfred Owen and so on) and then gives the titles of seven of his own books: *Rewards of Wonder*; *Dayspaces and Takings*; *Ridge Clay, Limestone*; *La Flandre, and By-Norton*; *Roman gone East*; *London seen Clear*; and *Fatigues and Magnificences*. We only know the first of these. The others were perhaps sent out, but to no effect. One can understand why this was so, because in the same letter of appeal, Gurney also asks for 'Free leave of crucifixion' and complains that 'they

Torture rack and insult so!' The quality of some of the writing may well have been missed in the dismay at such obvious disturbance.

There are different sorts of notebooks which survive in the Gurney Collection: there are fair copies, rough notes and working drafts. *Best poems* is the first type (though still with alterations, since Gurney was an inveterate corrector, usually by addition). It is a solid exercise book measuring nine by seven inches with a board cover of (now faded) brown and blue marbling and black tape binding; it cost one shilling and sixpence. It was written at some time between November 1925 and April 1926. It contains careful copies of poems in a consistent style and hand, mostly written on the recto and with relatively few alterations. This is a statement of where he is in the mid 1920s. It contains 65 poems, of which 15 were published in *Collected Poems* (not all in the same version); nineteen have been published in all.

The book of Five makings is more of a working manuscript, with various drafts and rethinkings in the same exercise book. It is the same type of solid exercise book as *Best poems*, with a board cover and a purple cloth spine; Marion Scott described it as 'the bright pink marbled book' though it too is now more faded; it cost two shillings. It is dated in Gurney's hand February 1925. Where *Best poems* is a position statement, this is Gurney at work, and may indeed represent five different occasions when he returned to it, the five 'makings' of the title. Three are obvious. First, as with the other text, there are copies onto the recto of the book. Second, several of these texts are completely redrafted on the facing page. Third, texts on the recto are enlarged by sections created on the facing verso and keyed into the existing text with arrows. Other returnings to the text, marked by pencil and different ink corrections, may make up the five makings. The book contains 52 poems, nine revised versions; twelve poems have been previously published. The present book thus contains two of Gurney's own collections, one of which represents his idea of completed work and the other gives an insight into his creative practice.

On the third of August 1915 Gurney wrote to Marion Scott, and in the course of the letter explained why he did not like a sonnet by Rupert Brooke:

It seems to me that Rupert Brooke would not have improved with age, would not have broadened, his manner has become a mannerism, both in r[h]ythm and diction. I do not like it. This is the kind of work which his older lesser inspiration would have produced. Great poets, great creators are not much influenced by immediate events; those must sink in to the very foundations and be absorbed (*Letters* p.29).

By the time Gurney came to write *Best poems* and *The book of Five makings*, the material which makes up most of the poetry had had time to sink in. Indeed the circumstances of his life in the asylum very rarely impinge on his poetry. He is more likely to respond in his poems to the title and spirit of a Whitman poem than to the walls around him. What he writes about is the war, the Elizabethans, Gloucester, France, London, people and places from his reading and his memory: the inhabitants and geography of his mind. All places had become like Gloucester had become during the war, when he wrote to Marion Scott on 27 July 1916 that 'Gloster, like Troy in Masefield's poem, has become a city in the soul' (*Letters* p.125).

One of the problems in reading the later Gurney is in avoiding the easy conclusion that any difficulty will be explained by the fact that he is in an asylum, that he is mentally disturbed. In other words the temptation on finding an obscurity in language or allusion is to make an excuse rather than an explanation. If the connections do not come easily, it is simple to assert that the reason is part of Gurney's mental problem. But this is to refuse to allow him to create poetry which is difficult, and it is undeniably true that both the language and the associations in these poems *are* at times difficult. He constructs a language and a pattern of allusions which he builds over several years, without a large public to question and test his work. As with Gerard Manley Hopkins, who published little in his lifetime, the lack of an audience accentuates the eccentricity. Gurney's difficulty is also as much the result of the way he was treated as it is a result of his condition. In the circumstances of the asylum he was starved of continuous intelligent communication, he was denied sustained intelligent response. This is not to say he was not treated according to the best lights of the day, nor that he was easy or helpful to those caring for him. In appeal after appeal he asks for a response, for publication, for consideration of his right to recognition for what he has done – '*First war poet*. (He does truly believe)' is written on his title page to *Best poems* and is a refrain frequently repeated. Now we see that there is some justification in the claim. But his letters were seldom posted; the response, of any sort, seldom came. And so he is left inside his own imagined world, with few regular visitors apart from the ever-faithful Marion Scott, with few fellow patients to whom he deemed it worthwhile to talk, with little contact with the doctors (significantly when Dr Davis struck up a closer rapport with him, his productivity seemed to soar; and Dr Anderson, who took over care of Gurney in May 1925, said that 'if he could be induced to talk about music or poetry he tended to become rather more capable of coherent conversation'. Quoted by William Trethowan in 'Ivor Gurney's Mental Illness'). In this imagined world, his contact is with the authors and subjects of his reading, with the stock of his memory, with the remembered landscape of his native county, and with the cities of his soul.

It is therefore no surprise that he is so enthusiastic about maps, those designs in which the reader can range over vast areas and across times. In 'Maps' (see below, p.130) he writes of the way he responds to lists, to maps, to names; the poem becomes a journey into a part-imagined and part-remembered land, and a celebration of his own ability to create: 'I watch their maps as my eyes watch books, or my own hand my heart leads.' In 'Sailor' he recognises that this is now the way in which he responds to people: 'When a sailor speaks to me my heart breaks / He turns an atlas' (p.49). It is characteristic of Gurney's mind and poetry in this period, as in his poem called 'Reference Map of the Civil War' (GA 21A.96-7), where he savours the names on the map and balances the exotic and distant against the familiar, where 'of Severn country I know the names even of stiles'. In a letter to Marion Scott of 16 August 1925 (GA 10.44), Gurney writes that 'I look at my little Atlas every morning'. In reading poetry of this period we have to be aware that we are following the complex diagram of Gurney's mind. His poem 'The Depths' sums up his escape through poetry:

Here no dreams touch me to colour
Sodden state of all-dolour:
No touch of peace, no creation
Felt, nor stir of divination.

Friend of stars, things, inky pages –
Knowing so many heritages
Of Britain old, or Roman newer;
Here all witchcrafts scar and skewer.

Coloured maps of Europe taking
And words of poets fine in making,
I march once more with hurt shoulders,
And scent the air, a friend with soldiers.

(CP p.167).

Gurney's imagined world deals in parallels and comparisons across time and space. He had always been ready to compare, say, Severn and Somme, and he finds it no more strange to compare contemporary and Roman, ancient Greek warrior and current cricketer, himself and Elizabethan or Jacobean dramatist. Thus some of the difficulties in juxtapositions and sudden leaps are simple parts of his way of thinking, emphasised by his circumstances. His language too, not a language in which he has to communicate very often or very seriously to those daily about him, becomes refined for his own purposes, not the purposes of common conversation. In daily communication with Jacobean drama or intense poetry, his language also becomes somewhat strange, a language for describing those things pressing on his own mind and for making them the 'escape from the worst / And most accurst of my woe' ('First poem', see below, p.91.)

Poetry was, after all, Gurney's lifeline, as it had been in the trenches. It provided structures which his life lacked; but his poetry is more a channelling of energy than a meticulously crafted design. On 4 May 1917, Gurney wrote to Marion Scott that

You will find that when I come to work again I also shall show much greater scrupulousness than before. It was simple lack of energy that kept me from revision, and the only method possible to me was to

write for a minute or two at top speed, refrain from tearing it up, and
return to the charge after some space of time. It won't be so after-
wards   (*Letters* p.252).

We can see in *The book of Five makings* how far Gurney was scrupulous,
and how far the pattern of his creative energy was to try again, to add,
rather than to adjust. It might well be said that Gurney reveals his
meaning not in the individual poem but in the bulk of his poems. He
continually circles back on experience, trying to find a new angle on it,
a new expression for it, a new direction in which it might lead.

It would be pleasant to think that Gurney is becoming better under-
stood and more fully acknowledged, and that this book will help in that
understanding. If that is so, his lines in 'Happy is he, Ulysses', a more
confident and contented poem than is usual in Gurney, have a
prophetic ring:

> I have come home, and Laventie is answered –
> The cold of Chaulnes paid, and long nights of Ypres on guard.
> Earth chose me – pain has paid for me – I shall have reward.

Select Bibliography

Ivor Gurney, *Severn & Somme* (Sidgwick & Jackson, 1917).

Ivor Gurney, *War's Embers* (Sidgwick & Jackson, 1919).

A.F. Barnes, M.C., *The Story of the 2/5th Battalion Gloucestershire Regiment 1914-1918* (Crypt House Press, Gloucester, 1930).

Poems by Ivor Gurney, principally selected from unpublished manuscripts with a memoir by Edmund Blunden (Hutchinson, 1954).

Poems of Ivor Gurney 1890-1937, with an Introduction by Edmund Blunden and a Bibliographical note by Leonard Clark (Chatto & Windus, 1973).

Michael Hurd, *The Ordeal of Ivor Gurney* (Oxford University Press, 1978). Referred to as *Ordeal.*

W.H. Trethowan, 'Ivor Gurney's Mental Illness,' *Music and Letters*, vol 62, nos 3–4, July/October, 1981.

Collected Poems of Ivor Gurney, chosen, edited and with an Introduction by P.J. Kavanagh (Oxford University Press, 1982). Referred to as *CP.*

Geoffrey Hill, 'Gurney's Hobby', *Essays in Criticism* vol 34, no 2, April, 1984.

Charles Tomlinson, 'Ivor Gurney's "Best poems"', *Times Literary Supplement*, 3 January 1986.

Severn & Somme and War's Embers, edited by R.K.R. Thornton (MidNAG/Carcanet, 1987).

Ivor Gurney: Selected Poems, selected and Introduced by P.J. Kavanagh (Oxford University Press, 1990).

Ivor Gurney: Collected Letters, edited by R.K.R. Thornton (MidNAG/Carcanet, 1991). Referred to as *Letters.*

Acknowledgements

We would like to thank Penny Ely, Trustee of the Gurney Estate, both for encouragement in our work and for permission to publish these poems. The original exercise books are both in the Gloucester Library: *The book of Five makings* at 64.2 in the Gurney Archive and *Best poems* at number 45457 in the Gloucestershire collection. The latter was acquired with the aid of the Museums and Galleries Commission and the V & A Purchase Grant Fund in July 1988. We would like to acknowledge the Library's support in the publication of these poems and thank the staff for their unfailing help in making the Gurney texts available, particularly Graham Baker, Susan Constance, Marian Fawlk, Dot Hawkins, Eileen Jeffs, Margaret Richards, Christine Turton and Helen Wright. We would like to thank Anne Buckley, Kay Baldwin and Julie Lockley for invaluable secretarial help. We would like to thank Harry Buglass for help with the maps and Bert Avery for help with Gloucestershire cricket history. And we would like to offer our personal thanks to Anne Johnson, Val Davison, Amy Thornton and Tom Thornton.

Chronology

This Chronology makes minor corrections to earlier chronologies but particularly concentrates on the period after 1920 to indicate what Gurney was publishing, how hard he was working, what were the ups and downs of his medical condition and what the context was for the two volumes which we print.

1890

28 August   Ivor Bertie Gurney born at 3 Queen Street, Gloucester, son of David Gurney, tailor, and Florence (née Lugg), the second of four children: Winifred (b. 1886), Ronald (b. 1894) and Dorothy (b. 1900). Alfred Hunter Cheesman acts as godfather at his christening.

1890s   Gurney family moves to 19 Barton Street, house and shop.

1896   Purchase of family piano.

1899   Joins choir of All Saints Church.

1900   Wins place in Gloucester Cathedral Choir and King's School.

1904   Sings with Madame Albani at Three Choirs Festival. Begins to write music.

1905   Begins close association with Cheesman and Margaret and Emily Hunt, who encourage his artistic talents.

1906   Articled pupil of Dr Herbert Brewer, organist of Gloucester Cathedral. Temporary posts as organist at Whitminster, Hempsted and at the

Mariner's Church in Gloucester. Forms friend-
ships with Herbert Howells, F.W. Harvey and John
Haines.

1907	Sits and passes matriculation examination at Durham University.
1911	Wins open scholarship to the Royal College of Music of £40 per annum. Cheesman provides another £40. Moves to London and takes digs in Fulham.
1911-1914	Student at the Royal College of Music. Makes acquaintance of Marion M. Scott and Ethel Voynich. Taught composition by Charles Villiers Stanford.
1913	Begins to write verse. Suffers from nervous prob- lems and dyspepsia diagnosed as 'neurasthenia' by Dr Harper. Recuperates at Framilode and Gloucester.
1913-1914	Writes the 'Elizas'.

1914

4 August	War declared on Germany. Gurney volunteers but is refused.
October	Takes post as organist at Christ Church, High Wycombe, where he makes the acquaintance of the Chapman family.

1915

9 February	Joins 5th Gloucester Reserve Battalion, the '2nd/5th Glosters'.
February	Battalion goes to Northampton.
April	Battalion goes to Chelmsford.

June	Battalion goes to Epping.
3 August	Sends Marion Scott the first poem of *Severn &* *Somme*.
August	Battalion returns to Chelmsford. Gurney redis- covers Whitman.

1916

19 February	Battalion moves to Tidworth and then on to Park House Camp on Salisbury Plain.
25 May	The 2nd/5th arrive in Le Havre. Travel to Le Sart.
31 May	Into trenches at Riez Bailleul.
8 June	Return to Le Sart, and move on to Laventie.
15 June	Relieve the 2nd/1st Bucks in Fauquissart-Laventie sector (relieved on 21 June).
27 June	Back at the Front for a week. Billets in La Gorgue followed by transfer to Richebourg-St Vaast.
6 July	Relieve Black Watch.
12 July	Relieve the 2nd/1st Bucks (relieved on 15 July) and move on to La Gorgue and Estaires.
19 July	In reserve at attack on Aubers Ridge.
August	Back to billets at La Gorgue.
9 August	In reserve. Sets John Masefield's 'By a Bierside'.
28 August	At Clearing Station having teeth attended to.
13 September	Out of hospital.
27 October	Battalion moves south to Albert and the Somme.
Early December	In Rest Station for 'cold in the stomach'.
9 December	Temporary job with water carts in Sanitary Section; what he calls the 'soft job'.

1917

Late January	Returns to normal duties.
7 February	Battalion marches to L'Etoile.
13 February	By train to Wiencourt, near Amiens.
15 February	To Framerville; relieve French infantry regiment in Ablaincourt sector.
March	To Brigade Reserve at Raincourt.

18 March	Battalion follows German withdrawal to Caulaincourt.
31 March	Battalion in Vermand.
7 April	Wounded in the upper arm; sent to Rouen.
5 May	Begins training again.
18 May	Back with the Battalion, which moves to the Arras front.
Early June	In the Line at Guemappe for eight days.
11 June	Out of the Line.
23 June	Rest at Buire-au-Bois and training. Gurney becomes platoon's crack shot.
14 July	Sidgwick & Jackson agree to publish a collection of Gurney's poems.
15 July	Transferred to Machine Gun Corps at Vaux.
31 July	Third Battle of Ypres (Passchendaele) begins. Gurney in reserve.
August	Battalion moves to Buysscheure and into support trenches near Poperinghe on the 21st.
10 September	Gassed at St Julien.
16–21 September	In hospital, correcting proofs of *Severn & Somme*.
22 September	On board ship to England.
25 September	In Edinburgh War Hospital, Bangour, where he meets Annie Nelson Drummond, a V.A.D. nurse.
6 November	Leave in London, High Wycombe and Gloucester.
15 November	Transferred to Seaton Delaval for signalling course.
16 November	*Severn & Somme* is published.

1918

12–18 February	Leave in Gloucester to visit sick father.
25 February	Examined for effects of gas and admitted to Newcastle General Hospital.
March	Moved to Brancepeth Castle, a convalescent depot.
28 March	Writes to Marion Scott telling her that he has spoken to 'the spirit of Beethoven', a sign of some kind of general nervous breakdown.

22 April	Moved to Newcastle General Hospital and on to Seaton Delaval.
8 May	Sent to Lord Derby's War Hospital, Warrington. Hospitals in the area pioneering the use of 'faradisation' – electrical charges – as a treatment for shell-shock, though no evidence of its use on Gurney.
19 June	Sends suicide note to Marion Scott. Tells superiors that he hears voices and wishes to be sent to an asylum.
4 July	Sent to Middlesex War Hospital, Napsbury, St. Albans.
4 October	Discharged from the army with a pension of 12 shillings a week. Not granted a full pension because condition 'aggravated but not caused by' the war. Returns to 19 Barton Street, Gloucester.
October	Working in a munitions factory. Friends and family worried by his erratic behaviour. Makes several attempts to go to sea.
11 November	Armistice Day. Finishes work at the munitions factory.
7 December	Poem published in the *Spectator*.
Late December	Goes to stay with Ethel Voynich in Cornwall.

1919

January	Returns to Royal College of Music. Ralph Vaughan Williams is his composition teacher. Moves into digs in West Kensington. *Severn & Somme* is reprinted.
22 February	Poem published in the *Spectator*.
25 February	Back at 19 Barton Street, correcting proofs of second volume for Sidgwick & Jackson, *War's Embers*.
3 March	Margaret Hunt dies.
22 April	Working at Dryhill Farm, Shurdington.
May	*War's Embers* is published.

10 May	His father, David Gurney, dies.
19 May	Living in St John's Wood, London.
August	Submits poems to the *Century*, the *Athenaeum*, *Harper's Magazine*, the *New Witness* and the *Spectator*, none of which are accepted. Goes on a walking tour of the Black Mountains with John Haines. Moves to High Wycombe on his return.
September	Takes post as organist at Christ Church, High Wycombe.
October	Suffering from 'nerves and an inability to think or write at all clearly'. Moving in London literary circles.
8 November	Visits John Masefield at Boar's Hill, Oxford, with F.W. Harvey.

1920

Late February	Walks from High Wycombe to Dryhill Farm via Oxford.
March	'The Twa Corbies' printed in *Music and Letters*.
May	Tries to set up home in a cottage at Cold Slad, Dryhill.
June–July	Two poems printed in the *R.C.M. Magazine*. Stainer & Bell publish 'Captain Stratton's Fancy'. Boosey & Hawkes publish 'Orpheus', 'Sleep', 'Tears', 'Under the Greenwood Tree' and 'Carol of the Skiddaw Yowes'.
October	Living in lodgings in Earls Court, London. Two poems published in *Music and Letters*.
6 November	Receives Government Grant of £120 a year, back-dated to 26 September. Meets Edmund Blunden and W.W. Gibson.
18 December	'Desire in Spring' printed in *The Chapbook*.

1921

	Chappell publish 'West Sussex Drinking Song'.

	Boosey & Hawkes publish 'I Will Go With My Father A-Ploughing'.
March	Boosey & Hawkes publish 'Since Thou, O Fondest and Truest'.
April	Living with his aunt at 1 Westfield Terrace, Longford, Gloucester. Unsuccessfully tries to get poems included in *Georgian Poetry 1920-1922*. Looks for and eventually finds farm work.
May	Two poems published by J.C. Squire in *Selections from Modern Poets*.
June–July	Living at the Five Alls, Stokenchurch, near High Wycombe.
Late July	Formally leaves the R.C.M. and returns to his aunt's house in Longford.
August	Works in a Cold Storage depot in Southwark for a fortnight.
Late August	Living with his aunt in Longford and doing farm work. Aware that 'something is more wrong than formerly'.
September	Winthrop Rogers publish 'The County Mayo' and 'The Bonnie Earl of Murray'. Describes himself as 'not yet well'.
October	Winthrop Rogers publish *Five Preludes for Piano*.
December	Obtains post playing the piano at a cinema in Bude. Retained for only a week.

1922

	Stanier & Bell publish 'Edward, Edward'. Boosey & Hawkes publish 'Come, O Come My Life's Delight'.
Early January	Living in Walham Green, London.
7 January	Poem printed in the *Gloucester Journal*.
Mid January	Living in Plumstead, London, and playing the piano in a cinema. Retained only for a fortnight.
February	Returns to his aunt's house in Longford. Looks for and finds farm work.

22 April	Poem printed in the *Gloucester Journal*.
May	Looking for a job in the Civil Service. Submits a volume of 80 poems to Sidgwick & Jackson, who return it, advising him to reduce and revise its contents. Loses third farm job in a month.
June	Finds work on a farm at Sandhurst hoeing wheat.
10 June	Poem printed in the *Gloucester Journal*. Resubmits poems to Sidgwick & Jackson.
30 June	Sidgwick & Jackson reject revised volume of poems.
July	'The Springs of Music' is published in the *Monthly Musical Record*.
3 July	Begins work at the Gloucester Tax Office but loses post after twelve weeks.
September	Moves in uninvited with Ronald Gurney and his wife at 52 Worcester Street, Gloucester. Behaviour is very disturbed and suicide attempts are made.
Late September	Goes to a Convalescent Home near Bristol. Condition does not improve.
28 September	Certified insane by Drs Soutar and Terry and admitted to Barnwood House, a private asylum in Gloucester.
October	Two poems printed in J.C. Squire's *London Mercury*.
21 October	Escapes but is recaptured after a few hours.
November	Writing the Barnwood House group of poems.
8 November	Escapes again but is recaptured at a police station.
21 December	Transferred to the City of London Mental Hospital at Dartford. Comes under the care of Dr Robinson, the Second Assistant Medical Officer.

1923

	Stainer & Bell publish *Five Western Watercolours;* and *Ludlow and Teme* as part of the Carnegie Collection of British Music.
January	Poem published in the *London Mercury*.

6 January	Escapes whilst walking in the hospital grounds.
6–8 January	Travels to London and visits J.C. Squire and Ralph Vaughan Williams, who informs the authorities. Returned to Dartford via Hounslow Infirmary.
February	Physical condition improves, but no change in his mental condition.
31 March	Poem published in the *Spectator*.
May	Poem published in the *London Mercury*.
June	Ronald Gurney sends his brother's manuscripts to Marion Scott. John Haines also gathering material.
August	Condition treated with Malarial injections, which have no effect on his mental state.
25–26 December	Entertains fellow-patients with his piano-playing during Christmas festivities.

1924

January	Six poems printed in the *London Mercury*. Receives seven visits from Dr Cyriax, an osteopath, for treatment for pains in the neck and head.
February	Receives books from Sidgwick & Jackson.
March	Refuses to get up from his bed in the verandah. Mental condition worse.
June	Supplied with music paper. 'The Western Playland' is copied out for the Trustees of the Carnegie Awards.
July	Reminiscences of Charles Villiers Stanford published in *Music and Letters*. Marion Scott arranges for Miss Mollie Hart to type out his poems and takes him out for a drive.
August	Sends out appeals listing seven manuscript books of poems that he wishes to have typed. Only one – 'Rewards of Wonder' – is now identifiable.
September	Supplied with music paper.
November	'Lights Out' published in the *London Mercury*. Three poems printed in *Second Selections from Modern Poets*. Writes to Annie Nelson Drummond

that he has completed '8 books' and has 'more new verses "Drum Taps"'.

December — Correcting typescripts of poems and writing new ones. Also writing song settings. Receives some French books.

1925

January — Prolific output of songs and poems, including a collection called 'To Hawthornden'.

February — Writes *The book of Five makings*. Receives music paper and writes four song settings.

March — Writes seven song settings, including three of French poems. Writes four collections of poetry and many single poems. Dr Robinson is replaced by Dr Randolph Davis, a Canadian with whom Gurney forms a rapport.

April — Poem printed in *Music and Letters*. Writes two collections of poetry and many single poems. Writes four song settings, including one to his own words called 'Song of the Canadian Soldiers'.

May — Dr Davis replaced by Dr Anderson. Writes some single poems and song settings.

June — Writes one collection of poetry and many single poems. Also receives music paper and writes seven songs. Taken out for tea by Marion Scott.

July — Receives music paper and writes five songs and one choral setting. Stainer & Bell publish 'Sowing'. Taken out for drives by Marion Scott.

August — Condition slightly improved. Writes several poems.

September — Receives music paper and writes eight song settings and some instrumental music. Also writes several poems. Taken out for drives by Marion Scott.

October — Writes one song setting. Marion Scott and Dr Davis discuss possible ways of treating Gurney's condition.

November	Receives music paper and completes one song setting. Writing poetry in the blue 'Marspen' exercise books.
mid-November	Marion Scott and Ralph Vaughan Williams make plans to transfer Gurney to Dr Davis's care as a private patient.
December	Writes three poems. Plan of handing Gurney over to Dr Davis abandoned.

1926

	Stainer & Bell publish *Lights Out*.
January	Writes a handful of poems and two song settings. Dr Hart, a Harley Street psychiatrist, is consulted about Gurney's condition.
February	Writing more poems.
March	Writes two song settings and a few poems. Taken out for a drive by Marion Scott.
April	Writes some poems and prose and a play called *The Tewkesbury Trial*. Taken to see a play at the Old Vic by Marion Scott.
Late April	*The Western Playland (and of sorrow)* published as part of the Carnegie Collection of British Music.
May–July	Writes a handful of poems. Taken out for drives by Marion Scott.
September	Writing poetry prolifically again. Mental condition worsens.
November	Writes two poems and much prose. Mental condition deteriorating; he becomes 'agitated' and states that he 'should be allowed to die'.
December	Severely deluded. Believes himself to be Shakespeare, Hilaire Belloc, Beethoven and Haydn, amongst others. Revises *A Midsummer Night's Dream*.

1927

| | Stainer & Bell publish 'Star Talk'. |

February	Treated by Mr Lidderdale, a Christian Science practitioner, on the advice of Adeline Vaughan Williams.
March	Provided with a table to work on in the hospital's gardens; 'does not desire to go for Motor Drives at present'. Treatment with Mr. Lidderdale continues.
April	Poem published in *Music and Letters*. Writes some prose. Mentally 'very confused'. Treatment with Mr Lidderdale terminated.
May	Revises and 'corrects' poems by Walt Whitman.
June	Becomes hostile to staff and fellow-patients and deteriorates physically.

1928

	Oxford University Press publish 'Walking Song', 'Desire in Spring', 'The Fields are Full', 'Severn Meadows', and 'The Twa Corbies'.
February	Gollancz consider publishing a collection of Gurney's poems. Marion Scott begins to collect material. Gurney's eyes are examined by an oculist.
June	Taken out for tea by Marion Scott.
July	Miss Mollie Hart types out Gurney's poems.

1929

January	Receives 'Brahms Sonatas'.
4 March	Taken to Gravesend and Rochester by Marion Scott. Wishes to buy a 'Phillips 1/- Atlas' but is unable to find one; Marion Scott buys him an edition of Shelley instead.
July–August	Taken out for drives by Marion Scott.
September	Taken out for a day trip in Dover by Marion Scott.
28 December	Visits the Old Vic with Marion Scott to see a performance of *A Midsummer Night's Dream*.

1930

Two poems published in *An Anthology of War Poems*. One poem published in *Jewels of Song*.

May   Taken on a day trip to Sheerness by Marion Scott.

1931

Two poems published in *The Mercury Book of Verse*.

1932

Visited by Helen Thomas, widow of Edward Thomas.

April   Taken for a drive by Marion Scott.
July   Taken for a drive by Marion Scott.
October   Taken on a day trip to Eltham by Marion Scott.
November   Two poems published by J.C. Squire in *Younger Poets of Today*.

1933

May   Condition deteriorates further.
December   Four poems printed in the *London Mercury*.

1934

January   Six poems printed in the *London Mercury*.
August   Six poems printed in the *London Mercury*.

1935

Gerald Finzi and Marion Scott make plans for the publication of a symposium on Gurney's work in *Music and Letters*.

1937

February   Gerald Finzi and Marion Scott proceed with plans for the publication of editions of Gurney's music and poetry.
April   Walter de la Mare agrees to write an introduction for an edition of Gurney's poems.

June	Gerald Finzi types out selections of Gurney's poems.
July	Becomes 'much weaker' physically and mentally.
23 November	Diagnosed as suffering from pleurisy and tuberculosis. Marion Scott urged to visit because he is in 'very poor health'.
26 November	Proofs of *Music and Letters* articles sent to him, but he is too ill to open them.
26 December	Dies from bilateral pulmonary tuberculosis.
31 December	Buried at Twigworth, Gloucestershire. Canon Cheesman takes the service.

1938

January	Symposium on his work appears in *Music and Letters*. Two volumes of his songs published by Oxford University Press.

A Note on the Text

Best Poems is a fair copy and *The book of Five makings* a working manuscript, and we have assumed that the reader would wish to see Gurney at work rather than have a 'tidied-up' text. We have therefore remained as close to the original as was compatible with clarity.

Deletions. Where there is a deletion we have transcribed the deletion if it is legible, or noted that it is there when it has been heavily crossed through. We have not noted false starts of a word finally chosen or alterations which merely correct the spelling or write out clearly a ~~word which he has felt might not be legible.~~

Insertions. Additional text which is written on the opposite page and marked for insertion by Gurney is inserted into the text and the line begun with an insertion mark: >. Other additions to the text are indicated by a slash before and after the insertion. These may be insertions before the line, above the line, or in a space left by the text. Gurney often makes use of any blank space to add a descriptive word which qualifies, expands or focuses the text, while at the same time compromising the original rhythm. It is not always possible to distinguish all additions when they are made in ink to a text written in ink and occupy a space which would have been blank in the original; but it is a fair generalisation to say that the first drafts are more regular than the poem when all its additions are included. Gurney seems to have valued truth and accuracy of observation above metrical regularity. In the text of *The book of Five makings* we have placed on facing pages the poem on the recto and its revision on the opposite verso.

Titles. Gurney usually underlined his titles and ended with a full stop, but not consistently. We have regularised his title style but kept the content and capitalisation.

Signatures. Gurney often signed every page of his manuscripts with name or initials, on one occasion in the middle of the poem. We have omitted the signatures.

We are conscious that the resulting text looks a little untidy, but the interference in its smooth running is deliberate, in order to remind the reader continually that these are poems in process, not always the finished work. But did Gurney ever regard anything as a finished work? His poems are almost always process towards.

BEST POEMS

Best poem of New
England
of City of Gloucester
of Embankment
of aldgate
City of Bristol
Tewkesbury.
others.

Ivor Gurney.

barnepie award, 1922-24
London Mercury. 1922-3
-4.
2/5 Gloucesters. 1915-1918.
First war poet
(He does truly
believe)

Detail of title page

Best poems *of New*
            England
            of City of Gloucester
            of Embankment
            of Aldgate
            City of Bristol
            Tewkesbury.
Ivor Gurney.   *Others.*

Carnegie Award, 1922-24
London Mercury, 1922-3
                    -4.
2/5 Gloucesters, 1915-1918
First war poet.
(He does truly
            believe)

To the memory of Alan Seeger

Marching hungry, marching hungry and weak,
After the Somme Line /(Winter)/, glad to be out of sick
Lands and packed billets, and nothing of /honest/ good.
Save by Aveluy, save by ~~the~~ /birch/ swamps and thin wood.
(I had dysentry and served only on Grandcourt line.
And a fatigue or two) ~~Year~~ Mild New Year's Eve ~~was mine~~ /had come
            benign/
By Crucifix Corner, and water carts there by me
Were filled – It was better on the chalk than with Infantry,
Rotting slowly to frozen heart in ~~the~~ thick mud.
Yet it tired – again we volunteered for the old Battallions –
Safety tired – they our friends in the battering and the guns.
We joined, marched past Albert and were on to South
When Belloy-en-Santerre /all shattered/ came noble to mouth –.
Roman, Roman; there was Cotswold /glimmer/ about the mind
That said Belloy-en-Santerre, metal clanged when men named
~~(But alas any human village should have had such wreckage~~
Sounds like hollow bronze. There they said an Alan Seeger
Had fallen – an American poet of France ~~in~~ /brave/ leaguer;
With the Foreign Legion taking /~~all~~/ a crack troops chances.
(A machine got him, soldier and poet – and his romances.)
An end of last strength marching, and rations bare – ~~meagre~~ meagre.
And there was an end of Staten Island, and New York City.
But I despised Yankee poets when the Gloucesters told me –
And as for pity – the Foreign Legion were outside of pity,
Who 'listed for soldiers chances and took luck's way.
(Gloucesters took Death's chances of Line and played the game.)
Carrying Walt Whitman in my haversack or at my back –
Or in a pocket – knowing nothing of Alan Seeger, name or fame.
Unless from a "Saturday Westminster", or "Times Supplementer."
I had already cut, and stuck in with potato fat
In my note book "I have a rendezvous with Death" with others
Of weekly papers, and scraps of verse that /some/ authors
Got grace of critic for – and ~~got out to~~ /sent post to/ France.

The last honour of poet, to be read in the mud smothers
Or dry heats of the Line. Alan Seeger was one of them –
But whether – cut out then or after, I cannot say – only
Walt Whitman was with me my thought as a sentry lonely.
Alan Seeger a name – though I might have known his poem.
The name forgotten – and his doom our equal chance doom.
Belloy en Santerre – and an American poet I knew nothing of.
But as for my own – they were written with labour or with love –
And once sent off, were out of my chance of my doom.
Expecting no printing, and my music /just/ so – well, just so –
Which wiser, I have known greater than the height most ages know.
Of height – Deaths praise for beauty and noble accusation.
And anothers hope of Cotswold stretched out in exultation.
These I thought nothing of – and /there/ more of the poem
The rendezvous, the foeman and the pictured blossom.
Who should have faced his meeting – and have walked on Staten
And known /written/ many a poem, and have known me – known me.
Brave enough; chucked by evil to an agony
By my own Land; a poet, and who wrote of Victory –
And made music – the chief sin of my own nation.
Against most high God – His spirit – , deep to forbidden damnation.
Ah, could his spirit have risen out of the grave to bring me
Where such unthought on evil might never sting me –
Or would his spirit walk free in Staten or Mannahattan;
To get a justice, or a pity – whose right nothing may righten.
For God most high requires such an honour of all human –
The honour of war poet as the honour of /first/ dawn or of /girl or/
        woman.

The Reward – and the earnings

There were not any rewards
Not promised to the soldiers
By Ypres or Laventie guards,
The Gloucesters, bolder and bolder…

As with the last strafe,
They found themselves not dead:
And in the terror the boy's laugh,
From the /crouched/ trench rose over head.

Or on fatigue, wrenching
The heart to last efforts.
There was not anything, anything
Denied of all life's rewards.

Happiness, employment, chance of work
Talk after the earning of living, –
All that a soldier come from ~~my~~ /mire/ and mirk,
Might require England of giving.

Night walking, music,
And the loved books to read
There by Richebourg, Neuve Chappelle –
Grandcourt – Vermand ~~and~~ Ypres ~~wall~~ gray–dead.
We took risks above the Roman will
Earned all honour, undenied.

To the City of Rome

What ruled Europe, and kept true honour of steel –
And built Cities where none were, and altered Cotswold,
Rose magnificent in the memory to metal and gold,
The Middle Ages rebirth of such past strength and noble; –
Holds all the heart of Europe – To Her pride we appeal,
Our wrongs, our claims of honour to Her must be told.
To redress the grievance of earths-right evil does withold,
And of arms, and song – Europe's wrong cries /out/ for Requital.

Rome known noble of so many generations of great ones,
Whose verse I have known, whose Camps walked at soft midnight –
To Her, a soldier and poet and maker in fight –
A singer, and celebration of a too dear paid

Victory – call out of a Hell of lies and pain as /once/ Virgil to the
        Sun.
Or as Plutarch to the virtue of heroes whose /true/ tales he made.

The Sudden Storm

Who but I walked the hills to see the lightning,
Say the few remembered things of Lear – the harried King,
Royal in his words, royal in his foul ruining.
Lightning at Framilode – and by Laventie trenches.
On Chilterns, and surely Cotswold – surely I have gone,
By road and rabbit run under the sudden sword shine;
Surely from Coopers and from Crickley the heavens have seen open?
But men have ceased reverence – and not honour those,
Braver or more bright of spirit who have hurried to the ways
Where great sound and great light fell in avalanches,
/Flat on the open slopes – or kept off by the branches./
Glorying the spirit to fulness, and great gladness of dark days.
(Beethoven shouting the delight out of the heart in high amaze.)
But West of Ypres we lying blanketed in the dark,
A sudden glow from Dunkerque made wonder, and the work –
And hunger-tired body rose up to guess at such storm,
Making no sound, in the September night calm and warm.
But next days papers told us, it was an electrical
Storm, for goodness knows what purpose let loose at all.
And no landing – or bombardment, or cause of excitement.
Anyway, sleep; but no sleep for me /possible/ there was
When the great electricity burst out in blaze,
By Chilterns, or Crickley Hill, or flat Longford's ways.

The Lightning Storm

Heavens fire bursts the clouds – the god of the air shows his moods
Or obediences – for no lightness in such indignation

Or in any light rain – is shown by the gods of the heavens –
Majesty fills all poetry's hearers with right floods.

But what shall I do, or say – whose wrongs cry to Heaven?
My right a Europes right, my wrongs of Europe's anger.
But though for a whim of conquest a nation make shout and clangour.
For an honour of God – that's mine – none breaks voice, silence even.

I saw French once

I saw French once – he was South Africa cavalry –
And a good leader, and a successful clever one to me.
A thought of Romance – for the thought of /war-/Veldt about him –
Who outwitted Boers – few could – who laid traps ~~without~~ /and got/
       him.
Egypt and Aldershot – Commander of the Forces.
And Mons Leader – and Ypres of the Worcestershires.
Now Captain of Deal Castle – so my book advises.
We were paraded for 6 mortal long hours of shoulders strain:
/And after hours of cleaning up of leather and brasses./
(O never, never may such trial be on soldiers again!)
And it was Winter of weather and bitter chill,
Outside of Tidworth on a barren chalk slope – Wiltshire Hill.
Six long hours we were frozen with heavy packs –
Brasses cleaned bright, biscuits in haversacks.
At last horses appeared hours late, and a Marshall
Dismounted, our shoulders so laden we were impartial
Whether he shot or praised us – Whether France of the Line
Or soft fatigues at Rouen, or Abbeville or Boulogne.
Slow along the ranks of stiff boys pained past right use –
Egypt and Veldt – Ulster – Mons, Ypres came;
And none to shout out of Ypres or cry his name –
Hell's pain and silence gripping our shoulders hard.
And none speaking – all stiff – in the knifed edged keen blast.
He neared me (Police used electricity) Ypres neared me,

The praiser of Worcestershires, Joffre's companion Captain he,
Who the Mèdaille-Militaire – the soldier honour of France wore.
Scanned me, racked of my shoulders, with kind fixed face
Passed, to such other tormented ones, pain-kept-in-place.
To stare so – and be satisfied with these young Gloucesters.
Who joined to serve, should have long ago seen Armentiéres
/Or Ypres, but at least Richebourg or near Arras./
But they would not send – youth kept us rotting in a town
Easy and discipline worried – better by far over by Ovillers –
Or Bethune – or St Omer – or Lys, Scarpe, those rivers.
/To keep a line better than march by meadow and down./
Chelmsford Army training to bitterness heart turning –
Without an honour – or a use – and such drear bad days.
Without body's use, or spirit's use – kept still to rot and laze.
Save when some long route march set our shoulders burning.
Blistered our heels – and for one day made body tired.
Anyway, on the chill slope – we saw Lord French ~~the~~ Commander ~~of~~
         on the hill –
Of short turf – and knew History and were nearer History.
Soon for scarred France – to find what Chance was to be feared.
To leave those damned Huts – and feel men in shell blast and shots.
To live belt-hungry – to freeze close in the narrow cuts
Of Trenches – to go desperate by barbed wire and stakes
And (fall not) keep an honour by the steel and the feel
Of the rifle wood kept hard in the clutch of the fingers, blood pale.

The coming of French after freezing so long on the slope.
Tidworth was Hell – men got Blighties – at least equal hope.
This was March – in May we were overseas at La Gorgues –
And the Welshmen took us, and were kind, past our hoping mind –
Signallers found romance past ~~their hoping~~ /believing/ of War's
         chance.
But the leader of Mons we had seen, and of History a mien.
South Africa and the first days, Mons, Ypres and between.

A London memory

Cleopatra builded an obelisk by great strength shielded
From weather or time wear.
By ~~the great strength~~ /stone's graniteness/ made noble and shaped at
      length
By long toil and dear labour.
But guessed not how the most magic minded of poet –
Should ever his best
Power to Her hour bring beauty into wonderfullest flower.
(Nor Antony, he guessed.)
But nearly two thousand years ~~I both wonders grand~~ /after, and three
      hundred after/
~~Of~~ These great Deaths had been –
I walked, knowing both, and of their wonder talked,
In June's night pure-serene.
Scraps of Enobabarbus and of Antony
The Galleon-captain of bad bravery,
Iras, and the Soothsayer and Philo's sorrow to see,
Antony but a Queens whim –
And that Spoiler of him –
Walking wasting his pride with loves soft glances dim.
But this was never known truly till the Town
Led me at length to steps in a narrow lane –
One still midnight of soft /gloom/ and cheek-kissing night.
There over Thames bright with strange coloured flames
(Their's are no names)
Wide to the further shore, and never lovelier more –
With barges and Thames –
Braving great piles set in the deep of the tide –
Ranged side by side;
Elizabethans and Venice – still Severn and String music
Together made poetic;
Perfect unfaltering beauty in shape moving or still –
Breathtaking beauty's will.
Sat for a while over the river and the /wet/ steps

(The dark water's laps.)
To think of Elizabethans their walking as comrades
Of craft, in the deep night – Great Bear high over their heads.
Or Capella or Milky Way or the loved Pleiads.
But there was not long before Lockharts light should show strong;
And tea with my books –
Be taken gratefully, watching the faces casually
Altering /their/ London looks.
But not so as to miss making if beauty says
Work, in my mind.
And not to miss Jonson, or Whitman, or /Charles/ Lamb his
Specimens – glory, to kind.
Or "*Spirit of Man*" – or Boswell the book one would rather than
The Empire Indian – to mind.
But tired not to think of music /Thames/ more till the dawn 'gan
            shrink
The dim veils from the sky.
Not any colour in imagination till the new work hours /time/,
Or new Thames of morning sigh high.
When Cleopatra's needle should show commoner in the days
Fulness and not magic at all,
An Embankment thing – not of Egypt Her matchless Queen,
But foreign there, nor noble.
And London lost to wonder, save in winter dawns under,
Mists ruddy, Light flooding full.

The County's Bastion

What looks far Bredon had, words to make said
Nothing are wanting; but will not square to place
Fall, – the poet is hurt – of tears /are/ his bread–
And takes his words, as pangs, as untold mischance.

But azure, and noble, like the thought of Rome –
Show under clear-after dawn – out Soft, like loves thought,

Bredon after night working showed from the home
I had, where Rome loved me – and to strict work brought.

Bredon, and Nottingham Hill, Cleeve, Crickley, and those
Sudden with new beauty, day after unlooked for day.
The poet might weep to have such thoughts, but well knows
Earth's poetry calls his pen; nothing his own of poetry.
Save God he follow, in simple spirit, till his lamp light goes.

After thoughts of fear

There is not anything of war but a soldier is proud –
(Save cruelty or a fear by after thought refused not allowed)
And of that War – so hard in its long endurance,
Its daily bravery; its passing Caesar's soldiers of Death's chance.
(I have read Plutarch – and know Rome's camps in the dark)
But though fears I had, that were bad to account for –
As by Tilleloy once, in day light a lost one to hunt for.
And running strafe messages /(desperate)/ from Tilleloy to
Fauquissart – hell and hell's racket /going/ through,
Or shaving at Richebourg holding the body straight –
(Till a shell burst the bays sandbags, just missed, a few feet …)
Or on fatigues at Grandcourt – or before the wires
Of Vermand, lying waiting for some hole, or some others
To get through, to get the whole business finished and done.
But a bullet got me, I saw not the end – To Rouen
Happy fate sent. Or the fear of Arras dusk, or Ypres,
That no pen says – and the soldier lies if he denies.
Fears beyond right /(unheld)/ in the night without sight –
Or in the threatening, air riving, dreadful day.
But the fear of beauty once shook me at Tilleloy
(Death's exaltation I made in a song of great joy)
And there was great fear of Heavens wonder at Robecq when West
Tumultuant in October glowed and exulted in such grandest
Ways, and the October trees rocked and blasted /hugely/ their best.

The fear of Aubers Orion – and of Varennes Orion,
The fear of Crucifix Corner looking out to the dim serene
Swamps and lovely silver birches of Aveluy's swamps.
The wonder and fear of Jupiter, Sirius, Venus, Heavens lamps,
And the wide, the wonderful all enveloping sacred dread
When Ypres dawned Her wide dawn unimaginably spread
In leagues unreckoned of height and width of first light –
Only the light thought on – and no grumbling said
To be stuck in mix of muds with the dreadfullest of jobs –
Hungry and weak and tired of the nagging of danger.
(Our thoughts of England died down from a love like anger.)
In late August or first September ~~before~~ /while/ the day still delayed –
And men before business thought of hot tea, and tobacco, and letters
                    to be read.

Honour

There is an honour of Europe all honour preserves,
That kept, the sacredness keeps purpose and never swerves –
The honour of war poet, mixed equal with blood and earth,
Not passionate to anger – the calm soldier, with God's right at birth.

By him, the Country is kept clear from false cheating peace –
By him, after war, vainglory is killed, and gratitude is
Kept by him, and his comrades for the stayers–at–home;
~~Who faced his dangers, and made song – will let no kept war's~~
                    ~~honour and~~
/Who having won Victory, will no bad thing allow therefrom./

Ford spoke a word

Late night, Ford sitting above the coal and wood,
Spoke to his friend – "I have never yet understood
How Shakespeare thinks – or comes to think /out/ his plays.

That are such poetry – and fit for all human ways.
Being born as Homer was ~~born to the~~ /god-born to/ use of the lyre –
Yet keeping well in with the gallery, and the poor small payer.
A happy talker, a listener to friends over his wine.
Happy with Jonson to be fighting over passage or line –
Yet with all admiration of so great a maker –
Only Gloucestershire forbids him distrust or fear;
He to the too-believing Scot as an acre
Of fruitful Gloucester soil to the mile or more of heather
Or granite – they say by Solway is the lands usual way.
Romeo and Antony, and the Henryies, and Timon his tragedy –
The sonnets which all men may differently love and see,
Speaking the heart out as David of Israels thought out.
These are not of any age, nor of common times degree, ...
Southwark houses, Stratford bore an Englishman of ages,
But I scrawl laboriously through my few hard pages,
And sit as late as he, but not so happy men say –
And take a hope from his dreams, (or Jonson's) strengths or rages.

Hazlitt

Hazlitt died, lying as he said "I have lived happy"
For a sad life was his if all tales be true;
Who worked so hard and well, and not much money came to,
Who walked in Wales, in Lakeland, and in Wiltshire way.
And wrote clean rapier prose, like best French unknown verse,
Clear English with an edge, cutting all ever superfluous.
And painted one true picture of Charles Lamb, so
England shall never be the same again that let go.
(A Venetian Senator, and our dear loved essay-writer.
But if he lived happy – it is well; for the happiness
He has given others, and English such touch and sureness
Will not be forgotten, though Fielding lie dust hid and rotten
(A master to[o] – and Scott's master) London would not
Be quite the same, had "Table Talk" missed to be written.

Or the news of Trafalgar's victory never had such note.
Stevenson crabbed his manner – Many have streamed his banner –

"The Times" and "The Daily News" are of his strict example.
And in strange places one may find honourable sample
Of writing – that from his ~~fire~~ /dark/ was gathered, from his flame lit.
Our walker, our late talker – friend in trouble, loved Hazlitt.

Ben Jonson

Few have praised the master of masters, who but I
Have right, that followed example, and did not lie
Idly between clean sheets when was work to do.
And saw Paul's tower by Embankment, high over City in dew
Not resolved; sunlight of hidden sun; and with apprentices
Drank, and watched faces in Whitefriars Lane, to my fancies.
Such work tops all but /of/ Shakespeare, the earths child, the sun's,
He /of/ no fairy gift, but of hard-fist resolutions –
And set to build as Bartholemews lover that Saint –
Or Wren in a later day raising great stone from the burnt
History and heart's love of the City London.
(So much merchants', scholars love so dreadfully undone.)
But if not I, that have praised in music his town
Worthy of his praise – and to glory made great stone known.
If not I that of Embankment and Aldgate wrote –
The Age is mean indeed, and honours only by rote.
Chapman, and Marston, Ford, Shirley, marks to frighten;
To frighten those, whom their example should urge and heighten.
The age is honourless, and my walking in loneliness.
My long thoughts in strict ways, my work – followings of him,
Are scorn to those whose lives are a wind breadth's whim.
Follow nor good nor evil – see not, with eyes custom dim.

Song

I had a girls fancies
At the pools;
Azure at many chances;
Limber rut holes –
Or shells at the dumps,
And a poets ~~gladness~~ /welcome/,
To see the night lamps
Of France, so like home.

But the girl in me went out
In Gommecourt trenches,
Minnewerfers – wooers stout
The only wenches.
And the poet died wholly
East of Vermand –
Before wires, and the bullet tears.
~~Too weak hungry to~~ /~~Puzzled, too weak to~~/ ~~stand~~
/Lying puzzled on wet land./

But the soldier kept both –
Saw Rouens blue river,
Tawny rock, high of faith;
And after Arras weather.
No blighty for a poet
No such luck for him –
Ypres dawns hurt his heart.
Flander's dusk dim.

Of Peasants

There have met me peasants by Maisemore road –
Poor, and proud never anything to have owed –
Ploughmen by Cranham – and Corse, and by Hartpury wood.
These all I have seen – admired, passed, watched the horses sheen;

Women folk, done in the house – standing of idle mood
At the cottage doors .... But in far France so I saw
Peasants of steelier will, not so acceptant a law
Of life – who took not earth, and man as they came –
But lit with inner spirit kept ever a flame.
(It turned to greed and avarice so writers said.)
But the old kindness of tenders, estaminet keepers,
The worshippers of Merville, and by Robecq poplars –
The faces of France du Nord – and Artois south –
Kept praise for ever natural to my English mouth.
Their wine, their kindness – and beer – cured English drouth.
Since – I have read French history and French poetry –
Found admiration heart deep– and know how came
The kindness of the coffee – and the crumbly bread.
The courteous serving of those /long/ tired of it – tired.
The unconquerableness – the carriage of the Gaulish head
Whereby Rome got a glory – And must well have persuaded –
My Cotswold mind watching their French soul was all fired.

Of Grandcourt

Through miles of mud we travelled, and by sick valleys –
The Valley of Death at last – most evil alleys.
To Grandcourt trenches reserve – and the hells name it did deserve.
Rain there was – Tired and weak I was, glad for an end.
But one spoke to me – one I liked well as friend –
"Lets volunteer for the Front line – many others wont".
"I'll volunteer – its better being there than here".
But I had seen too many ditches and stood too long
Feeling my feet freeze, and my shoulders ache with the strong
Pull of equipment – and too much use of pain and strain
Besides he was Lance Corporal and might be full Corporal,
Before the next straw resting might come again.
Before the next billet should hum with talk and song.
Stars looked as well from second as from first line holes.

There were fatigues for change, and a thought less danger –
But five or six there were followed Army with their souls –
Took five days dripping rain without let or finish again –
With dysentery and bodys of heroic ghouls.
Till at last their hearts feared nothing of the brazen anger,
(Perhaps of death little) but once more again to drop on straw bed-
        serving
And to have heaven of dry feeling after the damps and fouls.

May the companion

May was a companion of mine – I had light body –
No more fear than of Regulus I had of this girl or prince –
Night walker, who loved cold water on his dear flesh; fearlessly
Facing the innocentest first morning as equal as he.

Only – what died not in him – for the dusk quickened into
New beauty – the living dark – drew to the midnights change
Altered in me – I had need of my books, pen and range
Of thought in the lit room – Nature's love died to making, hard-set
        determined rue.

On the First Army

They were trained and paid for soldiers for long years –
Before the earth of France touched their boot leathers.
That the beginning would be hot, they well foreguessed,
But trusted to Peninsula and South Africa for the rest.

Whose soldier pride was ~~set~~ /posted/ to freeze /still/ in pools –
No shots, or bayonets, they kept Ypres with frozen souls.
Only the Territorials, who kept Gommecourt or Laventie walls
Know honour enough for those who must for reputation face
No mans with bullets in rows – and still wire – we in place
With no reputation: as brave as Cotswold when Rome in morning calls.

O Tan-faced Prairie Boy

O friend who took an ~~extra~~ /double/ stand for me –
Signaller, who white faced, stayed on post never disgraced,
Buzzing and tapping messages in the strafe's devil's-glee –
And walked by Crucifix Corner, and the canal still in summer.
Was almost smashed when the mine went up by Tilleloy the malign –
And got to Blighty, and was officer (and got honour of degree)
And you who gave me kindness and lies at Chaulnes –
And you, true Gloucester, of whom Ypres has the bones.
~~A Company almost of true friends tried to the courage' ends –~~
The dead with living equal – and living lucky alone.
(Having taken Dead Man's many chances and still ~~being~~ for other ones)
A verse of love for you – and the others who chattered
Gloucester and talk of girls when the shrapnel shattered,
And cursed a fate that had ~~no~~ /never/ wine nor beer;
That is not less than six kilometres, and perhaps farther;
Love endless for you – though I win to rapt, and mapped
Music, and to my deep thought get great sound shaped.
You knew my mind – what it hoped – not to keep body unhurt –
~~But~~ Nor to save life so much as to return to the heart;
To find my heart again in some candle lit room,
And work out music till the true shape and soul should come.
I left not you – why have you left me to fall
Into the hands of evil lying lies to the truth of Hell.
(I was a war poet, England bound to honour by Her blood)
Why have you dead ones not saved me – You dead ones not helped well?
Or is it even Michael, my master, strict; forbidding a good?
But why you, Gloucesters, O dead ones, my dear companions,
Laventie – Vermand – Ypres, why have you not given
Courage from beyond the grave to your comrade so driven
By torment from his heart to call for you, friends under the guns?

Is there not honour of war poet at rebirth, or in Heaven?

After Sunset

"I'm seventeen come Sunday" I have heard by /West/ Gloucester way.
A girl sang it, /chance-by/ the freshness and earths-thought of May.
Laventie trenches, the first hearing of the /dear/ lamenting
Of David of the White Rock – when the first sickness took him –
        only Death wanting.

And by Chelmsford – the Farmer's boy in great swinging chorus.
There was Danbury Hill – or hell's length of one road before us —
That led to the ranges – no road ever half so long – not ever;
~~And~~ in Chiltern nights myself /beer tasting/ have made country song.

But what of "Tarry Trowsers" that none else /(unhappy)/ knew?
Or "Farewell lads" with its B natural – spirit fresh as /young/ dew?
~~The~~ men that ploughed ~~the~~ brown lands /with strong hands/ had
        they no honour
Of earth? Was there no love of the free air behind the cottage door?

And there was a song of Scotland /loved/ I heard on a soft
Job in Picardy that set the heart soaring aloft to moor and croft,
Drew fire, and tears, and pictures, and set me to making – again,
By Aveluy – where the Crucifix was – and the Scots – with musics
        own heart aching again.

The First Violets

She had such love and after my music sent
Me out to the woodlands, and to wander by meadow or bent
Lanes of Severn – I got them all into my music –
I would wander my soul full of air, and return to her quick.

Wandering was four miles an hour – and caressing stray brambles –
With love of earth and God – and sacred friendliest grumbles
At God, Who would not grant such great work as to Beethoven came –
That felt not such air – nor had such a love of clear flame.

By Highnam I saw them – and wet of brow by Prinknash –
Maisemore, and Corse Hill in streams loving water dash.
They mixed with "Winters Tale" in my mind, and songs core,
That Vienna loved, and felt move in the hot room country lore.

Gloucestershire's air made /clear/ loveliest wrapping of heart.
She blessed it, and took with one touch the foldings apart
Who was love and music and companionship and most dear
Work-thought in the clear room with the Bechstein and Holbein there.

~~Drum taps~~

The noble rattle of the drums at the Town Northampton
Has long stayed with me – as of Wagner or as of Beethoven.
The drummers with no packs marching with so ~~noble~~ /steady/ a
              rhythm,
And sharp sound setting the feet going – and the spirit with them.
So noble a call of parchment and wood not long kept good.
Chelmsford had it seldom – Epping I not remember,
And on Salisbury plain – in Spring weather /bleak/ like December,
Another drum call ~~there was~~ /weak as a childs/ ; and many bugles
But not that satisfying drum masterpiece after inspection's ill ease.
And in France, nor drum nor bugle I remember, save once
When in the trenches, before the others were going hence
A full two hours – and a signaller had his privileges.
Down by Riez Bailleul a bugler sounded (Romance pages)
As of a tale – "Retreat" – after days dust and heat.
In the afterglow, while the signallers were almost ready to go.
A good poem – "Hail and Farewell" – I was moved to, and made of it.

City of Ships

O London Town, you whose Dome has looked down
A three centuries on the history the new Church thought on most –
Did you send boys, who had men enough for a worlds renown,

To face the Ypres terror – Gloucesters white as a ghost?
And expect victory of those you shirked your Duty theron?

Marryat would have cursed ~~your~~ /you for/ evillest greed.
Dickens would have flamed high, and dashed off a screed.
Fielding, and /George/ Borrow – Your boys kept men from sorrow,
Or even anxiety – good wages, and war News to read.

~~Dirge for~~ /Picture of/ two Veterans

We liked you, but you got frost-feet went down too soon;
You took the lightest bags, and did fatigue, leaving alone
Line Service – with a trust in Providence heavy or your platoon.

Well, you had your way, and Grandcourt finished your service.
(You would have held and died, but your place with your families.)
Yours was no frame for Vermand or dreadful-earth Ypres.

You passed down trench – and got to the Dressing station;
We granted you right (and envy) to your right elation,
Who stayed and expected parcels from a grateful nation.

But got few – Base pinched some – and /sly/ Transport /the/
          candles,
They got to us ragged, with neither string straight nor handles.
And you had plenty in Blighty, and bread in bundles.

Dirge for two striplings

God knows the eyes of one were steady and bright,
A company's delight –
And mine watching silent, the business of a poet.
The other of Gloucester born, that was so men say, the one
God like County of England – of all England.
He cursed his men and our men at Ypres and died,
Being sweet and tender hearted and all-brave beside.

What tears by Blythe, what hurt by Severn there was,
Is for the guess, but only our Gloucester Company's guess.
That had kindliness, and sweetness of heart, and grace.
For all their long marching, and endurance, Courage without praise.
Courtesy in billets, and nice manners in farm or estaminets.
The Severn Valley goodness coming out in courteous ways.
And as for the North – the miners with small food kept –
Would make a feed for soldiers while their hunger slept –
With bright flame, and all giving generousness, and a recklessness of
        living,
~~As in dying one had – with no blot on them, and goodness to amaze.~~

I saw Her soul

She was a thought of 'prentices talking till dawn,
And I had seen the steps,
And gone by Aldgate, and Westminsters long
Stretch to watching the shifting lights, ~~and~~ like Bartholomew maps,
And stood on London Bridge, at strength wondering, and long ages –
Knowing Borrow only, not Carlyle his clearest, white pages.
So to Whitefriars Lane,with tea drinking desires,
Tired body, books in my pocket, ~~and~~ /Lamb, Bridges Whitman –/
To the street of "Daily News" and Lockharts dim glows,
To push the half doors – and smell the steam ~~and~~ /of tea and/ kippers.
(Hating as makers will, the thought of food still.)
Only pain drove me to eat, to the undoing, not thinking
Of work – how should the spirit think in heaviness of body?
So in the first dawn, others asleep in lazy beds, linking
A sixteen hour awake – to an eight asleep;
Knew not as I knew how John Fountain made words weep;
Or watched quick London faces, to all speech ever ready.
Who had served soldier maybe – and were of trenches thinking
(Maybe) the silent ones – in their still silence of dreams;
Before the setting of type – or the set job finished.

Sailor

When a sailor speaks to me my heart breaks
He turns an atlas, of voyage and parrots speaks,
Of sea delay – and of Russia, and fevers way.
I can sail boat, have seen water, ~~and~~ /in green/ white foam.
From Minsterworth to Newnham sailed, and to Framilode home,
Hit sand, and cursed Her leaks, hit rocks and mended,
With painful care slabbing tar, and oakum, wood squares there.
And taking doubtful water again, finding she'd hold.
(The great sail shining high against azure with wide gold.)
And after to tea, returning (to dodge eating)
By Rudford, and Longney and above Priding beating and beating –
The sands and the shallows and stones my eager hating.
But after I came to a war poets, right and more,
Of maker by Severn and Thames, Her midnight shore,
Yet England has denied me pity and right and all beside the
Honour is mine – who was loving and life-reckless sailor.

The Silent One

Who died on the wires, and hung there, one of two –
Who for his hours of life had chattered through
Infinite lovely chatter of Bucks accent;
Yet faced unbroken wires; stepped over, and went,
A noble fool, faithful to his stripes – and ended.
But I weak, hungry, and willing only for the chance
Of line – to fight in the line, lay down under unbroken
Wires, and saw the flashes, and kept unshaken.
Till the politest voice – a finicking accent, said:
"Do you think you might crawl through there; ~~Gurney~~ theres a hole;"
                In the afraid
Darkness, shot at; I smiled, as politely replied –
"I'm afraid not, Sir." There was no hole, no way to be seen,
Nothing but chance of death, after tearing of clothes

Kept flat, and watched the darkness, hearing bullets whizzing –
And thought of music – and swore deep heart's deep oaths.
(Polite to God –) and retreated and came on again.
Again retreated – and a second time faced the screen.

Scabious and Trefoil

Out of the dun turf on the high Cotswold they grow,
Whether before Roman, or of high Roman memory
I know not; only the nobleness of them /fills/ minds so –
Of the cohorts who guarded there, and of Latium or Tuscany.

Trefoil thats nobler than the steely sword.
Scabious more Roman than the page of ordered
Sound like set metal; and on Crickley to guard
Inner England from the gold Wales seen far bordered.

Plutarch was my work friend – a scrap of Catullus
Nearly my all Latin, but by right of blood,
Mixed of Roman, Briton and Gaul, I climbed high to the sentinels
Deserted walk, and felt the night winds and shades go by.

Rome was my friend, long earned of nightwalking and strict
Dedication – the music of strings from the Rhine side begotten –
These were my Rome; and though the sentry walk were derelict,
Well I had knowledge of soldiers thought – Ypres has not forgotten.

But at Ypres were no scabious, at Vermand Trefoil /was/ none.
The soldiers thought kept alive by more courage than cohorts
Needed, ever; their thoughts easy out to Adriatic gone.
The Terror needed mastery, Flanders hurt and tested all hearts.

June brought scabious in noble single half azure signs,
Drawing thought out to music, or the dear book of Lorraine
and Nancy, the Great vat, the sun-glory; casual meetings –
A baker, a scolding mother, Alps worshipped without stain.

Trefoil – another book of Parnesius and / of / D'Aquila –

Maximus and Hanno – the boys book of the grown man;
Tenderly touched keys of the loved piano, where for a day
I might find Rome's heart in fugue or Quartett, never undone.

Clear in the high morning on the dim untrodden
(Save of unhurting sheep) turf of the slope never done
For wonders newness; a boy would make all forgotten
~~The~~ With rapt communing dreaming close to the spirit Roman.

June would find me there, scabious would salute, trefoil
Take my most precious tenderness, with a gift of tune
Home would find later – September misted lovely past tell,
Grim-lipped January found me wandering under ~~the~~ half height
        moon.

Dead trefoil trod under my quick feet under January's stars,
Scabious gave way (poor stalk) to my clear blood tread,
Romans my friends, as from ~~I~~ earth I had, and midnight masters
Knowledge, let kindly thought on me – their darling, though dead.

Rhyming words, what raised Crickley passes out of ~~the~~ flesh soon,
Takes refuge in woman, and [deletion] /after is bright/ stripling, to
        touch
The soldiers armour, ~~to guard for Rome~~ /see clearer scabious/ and
        trefoil than overdone
Sentinels, mind tired with custom and the day by day of watch.

The room of two candles

Music tells love–
I have told you my love in music,
Are you not content my heart to have drawn to far smart?
The touch of keys as subtle as the flame in my heart,
You still there with your quiet face, and all love in thoughts light.
There is no use in tales, girl, please, quick:
It is so little to give.

You are so right
In your aloof pride, ~~and your~~ you keep your way so
Never, so as to give a hold for one word to uphold
Any hope of mine – and a kiss must for an age be told
To ones own heart enough, and such frail human stuff
That needs a touch of lips for an hour of woe –
Small pay: pain great.

Not any touch?
Well, to the quiet keys I must return
Out of their dumbness, beauty shall speak better than all
(Save kisses) Save kisses; and day's beauty ~~say what this is~~/brought to
          call/
Of some poet had his pay of grief well in his day,
But caught June morning virgin to nights beauty:
She willing: of love as much.

Iliad and Badminton

Men hurl no more the quoits, or bend bow in Tothill
Fields, but a sight of Jessop at his crouch and act –
Stays with me still, though my arm with the rudder have racked.
Shot a hole through a German maybe, Vermands hill.
Hobbs and Strudwick – they keep the /long/ thoughts like Shirley
Of so clear line – and of Boswell, I saw the burly
Past Cricket figure of him, W.G. of Graces.
Out soon – a venerable figure – ~~slow of paces~~ as from Froissart merely;
Hector was valiant all, but Townsend defied courage,
Would glide where Hector smote, not noted ever on page.
They talk of Kreisler and Ranjitshinjhi, both princes.
Delicatest /McNeill/ Whistler; etching like Paliaret surely –
Glory enough for one – neither glory for others nor wage.
From dead Shrewsbury, as from the younger Grace memory winces –
But Gloucester, Cheltenham's way, with August stays clearly;
Troilus walks white, Cressida truer watches him;

Agamemnon takes brute ease in the half crown gallery –
Priam tells tales of Merton, Thornbury, – doleful since his
Brothers of Troilus – loved son – finished dim
His sight by Richebourg – and bats no more fourth man,
Or takes a bowling turn, drawing eyes of Helen.

Afterwards

When watching faces in the smoke gone blue
Of public houses – to the ceiling half seen;
They were like the ~~faces~~ /looks/ of Smith, or Robinson, or Green,
That got the wound, or died ere the thought had been.

My silent love that feared the pride work gives men,
(Yet I a nightwalker) they shared not love –
Watched glass to mouth in slow line and uptilt move;
Heard voices as by Laventie tell gossip again.

Whose fault? – (they'd not be friends). Only the soldiers ~~heart~~
          /heart/
Had done braver things than many – though poet *there both*,
Hurt with the thought that he who sang longing and wrath
Of soldiers, should in the friendly Inn, be kept dumb, apart.

Lance Corporal

He would go out to shoot a September brood
Of birds that settled just in front of our mud
And sand bag, frost and corrugated iron accursed homes.
He would go out on search parties, and at least touch wood.
(So'd I , when I learnt what sleep was allowed after that – after that.
To risk a wound, and sleep like a log, sheet surround.)
His was a happy nature, in the flat
And planted Flanders, as in high Cotswold;
Heart and soul would give niceness like largesse gold.

He hurt me once or twice; but his goodness passed
All that was fair – and my book was his praise at last –
He thanked I liked Gloucester boys as much as he;
Cursed me at Ypres for leaving the Company;
Needless – I was longer in – and with no more writing;
In front of Gloucesters, and better moving with
Infantry, Gloucesters that would live and let live.
Didnt go over the top, but would have gladly gone –
Since double as long in the line was the price there known.
Glad for return – promise to the old Battallion –
Not to see, hear of – or touch a triple damned machine gun.
That promised to be interesting, and nothing so dull –
That promised to be safe – and with line's length double,
And fatigues like hailstorms for shrapnel, and four mile long.
And safety – that had no candles – and no route marching.
He died there. (I nearly died) and gas got me home;
Glad am I to think, for his memory's sake, how the trouble
Of spirit vanished, when the promise was given of return
To our battallions – with going over in Hell's down-come,
Hells shatter of steel, but fair does of time in the line.
And freer moving, and pride of a Ypres soldier.
(But winter coming on – worse than frost bite colder.)

[Untitled]

"Girl, girl why look you so white?
Is it death has you taken?"
"No, no, You must not question me so.
"Out of the air is this shaken."

"Sickness out of the air can be cured
"By simples or one night in the open.
"But on you – heart's threat so as you stared.
"Some power for you bad forelooking has shapen."

"It is my dead love, who whispers me now.

"I loved him well. I love you far better.
– "That is not borne; anger, hurting, and scorn,
I can take, but not to be of Love the debtor "

Yes, but for my love of him, he has called
Me to his side, quick as maybe.
It was never so – It is lies: so enthralled
Never I was, whate'er days /tale/ be.

My own heart's master I was, and he
The taker of what I chose spared
Out of the richness of my fancies [deletion] (much less
Of his worth) I dared.

Shall the dead leave the deep clay to mind
The living of a love year covered?
Does death presume so? And out of the blind
World of spirit a known one hovered."

"Dear, let deny your heart, come kiss
That past love out of fancy until
He as the morning mist on our hill
Of delight be, bathed in sun bliss.

"Dear, let the dead one let you rest.
My heart is as rich with earths love,
Loving with poetry from the upturned fresh
Ploughland, with small weeds above.

He had no more – let the terror slide out
Of your eyes and heart – I too, beloved
Of earth – have such right of
Honour of the soul, delight of
Earth, you should be moved."

Though your girl's virginal naturalness
To the secretest wood be dear.
(Or the ploughland) there are gods [deletion] shall confess
I, too the poet, have right here.

May and September, the clear, the romance-one –
Put fear away.
That you have unfaithful been or looked deathly…
~~Of~~ /To/ the Earth's Yea or Nay.

Only put out the blind terror from eyes,
For one by dear earth chosen
For service, poetry, and love's ways
Of reward for service and for night seeking.
Wandering to music's heart after the day's
Common wonder (but never losen)
~~The common wonder of wandering and making.~~
Make love for me your solace for eyes
Feared awhile, and be calm to admire and see.
There's evil in death does so awaken.

Birds

There were small birds would fly in the trenches at times,
Loved to our Gloucester eyes –
Who would see with surprise
Some visitor from home with a touch of rhymes
Ending a talk and poetry becoming easy and wise.
These were the hedge sparrows /(music)/ by Maisemore, Her green
Small hill, and Minsterworth starlings flocking in clouds
Of whirring black ones on the gold stubble and half seen
Lovely weeds of hearts ease, pimpernel, ladies bedstraw.
Blackbirds of Wellington Street; martins of Leadon's law,
One kingfisher, one laughing linnet in the shrouds
Of April, under the luminous azure white heaven's measure.
Linnets with wavering flight going over Corse way to delight
Boy with as sure
A sense of earth as any of ~~the~~ birds – but earths friend and more
So some good Spirit friended to the music or verse ended.
There was a yellow hammer by Hartpury manor

And robins by High Hartbury were good as crumbs to me.
(Had I been robin – or yellow hammer a loving human.)
(If crumbs are dear to robins like the heart's touch of humans)
~~Or~~ They were my brothers, but I a prince above others,
Having music within my blood, verse eager to say my mood.
The fire of sword and steel shine with pity of a woman.

Greene

Greene, was he truly imprisoned, I have read him in Morley:
A clear poet enough, and Shakespeare's master surely.
His lovely lines I know – but seven years for debt?
They must have let him out daily to talk hot
Of verse over drink some actor, fearing God, gave clearly.
To talk, and beg his right honour of denying poets –
Entreat salvation from the four walls set – square set.
But where's his book on book of prison notes,
What said Ben Jonson so good a man went down?
Could Marston or Ford, not spare a few wretched groats?
Was there not poetry to be thanked for by some woman –
Who yet could honour steel and the maker's great virtue –
"Master Shakespeare has a country blood, and should feel
With kindliest spirit – Master Jonson comes from the gray
North, that great good one, Master Chapman from Hertford way.
It is a great shame that rich one – and that great scholar –
And the Greek gentleman whose fame of Iliad /alone/ shall stay
(They say) to leave Robert Greene in a cellar
Or store room, to curse all London, poets, scholars whatever
For damned ungratefulness, and no honour; and no pleasure, never.
A poet if ever was – and for mere money fallen in disgrace.

The noble wars of Troy

That was not of Laventie or the ditch of Grandcourt,
But Kings School football, and the sail taut by Rudfords farm court –
I knew it walking Portway hard so the blood sang tunes,
My eyes searching shadows, and better of light than the moon's

Water – I battled with water – Earth – I have dug earth – where
Salisbury Plain falls to Stonehenge in a level clear –
Air? It was my comrade, like light, or music.
Leadon, or Longford, the Cairn – those have known me – my step.

Bathed in Octobers Severn, muddied with Picardy –
Kissed by the June wind on high Coopers looking to Severn Sea;
Beloved child of the ploughland and the grassy fallows –
There was no gift Briton or Roman denied me of love that all hallows.

Hector I knew of Southwark, and of Buckley's pages –
Wrestled with Chapman, and took eternal golden wages.
Troilus in the January night wondering at Orion and never
Able to understand half such a wonder of high beauty – not ever.
My friends of Greece or Rome, Cotswold my two thousand years home.

Christmas Night

High in the divine night the winter stars
Keep thought of Christmas, and I, of all Gloucester alone
Reading Hardy awhile, before my desires
Fire to music (or move) and more making out to action gone.

Orion that at Varennes and in Essex I saw –
(Immortally worshipped in great Beethoven's music)
The Pleiads somewhere; they always were, and the flow
Of Milky Way on Heaven; Hardy my mind made critic

Seeing so well such square form; and that must set
Past Orions power or far Cotswolds the hand and the spirit

Shaping of sound, manors or abbeys of sounds set –
Hoping a reward of praise, and unborn praise to inherit.

Overhead, the people slept, outside the far heavens crept,
Noel came to pass, and there was no bird of dawning
To fright ill spirits from the land all past love kept –
Briton, Roman, Dane, and Elizabethan; yearning
As men will to the Atlantic earth, and the love deep of Rome that slept.

Felling a tree

The surge of spirit that goes with using an axe,
The first heat – and calming down till the stiff back's
Unease passed, and the hot moisture came on body.
There under banks of Dane and Roman with the golden
Imperial coloured flower, whose name is lost to me –
Hewing the trunk desperately with upward strokes;
Seeing the chips fly – (It was at shoulder height, the trunk.)
The green go, and the white appear –
Who should have been making music, but this had to be done
To earn a cottage shelter, and milk, and a little bread;
To right a body, beautiful as water and honour could make one –
And like the soldier lithe of body in the foremost rank
I stood there, muscle stiff, free of arm, working out fear.
Glad it was the ash tree's hardness not /of/ the oak's, /of/ the iron
            oak.
Sweat dripped from me – but there was no stay and the echoing bank
Sent back sharp sounds of hacking and of true straight woodcraft.
Some Roman from the pinewood caught memory and laughed.
Hit, crack, and false aim, echoed from the ampitheatre
Of what was Roman before Romulus drew shoulder of Remus
Nearer his own – or Fabius won his salvation of victories.
In resting I thought of the hidden farm and Romes hidden mild yoke
Still on the Gloucester heart strong after love's-fill of centuries.
For all the happy, or the quiet Severn or Leadon streams.

Pondered on music's deep truth, poetry's form or metre.
Rested – and took a thought and struck onward again,
Who had frozen by Chaulnes out of all caring of pain –
Learnt Roman fortitude at Laventie or Ypres,
Saw bright edge bury dull in the beautiful wood,
Touched splinters so wonderful – half through and soon to come down
From that ledge of rock under harebell, the yellow flower – the pine
          wood's crown.
Four inches more – and I should hear the crash and great thunder
Of an ash Crickley had loved for a century, and kept Her own.
Thoughts of soldier and musician gathered to me –
The desire of conquest ran in my blood, went through me –
There was a battle in my spirit and my blood shared it –
Maisemore – and Gloucester bred me– and Cotswold reared it,
This great tree standing nobly in the July's day ~~great~~ /full/ light –
Nearly to fall – my courage broke – and gathered – my breath feared it,
My heart – and again I struck, again the splinters and steelglinters
Dazzled my eyes – and the pain and the desperation and near victory
Carried me onwards – there were exultations and mockings sunward.
Sheer courage, as of boatsailings in Equinoctial unsafe squalls
Stiffened my virtue – and the thing was done. No. Dropped my body –
The axe dropped – for a minute, taking breath, and gathering the
          greedy
Courage – looking for rest to the farm and gray loose piled walls –
Rising like Troilus to the first word of "Ready" –
The last desperate onslaught – took the two inches of too steady
Trunk – on the rock edge it lurched, ~~near~~ threatening my labouring
          life –
(Nearly on me) Like Trafalgars own sails imperiously moving to defeat
Across the wide sky unexpected ~~sailed~~ /glided/ and the high bank's
          pines and fall ~~straight~~ straight,
Lower and lower till the crashing of the fellow trees made strife –
The thud of Earth, and the full tree lying low in state –
With all its glory of life and sap quick in the veins…
Such beauty, for the farm fires and heat against chilly rains.
Golden glows in the kitchen from what a century made great…

The axe fell from my hand, and I was proud of my hand,
Crickley forgave for Her nobleness, the common fate of trees.
As noble or more noble, the oak, the elm that is treacherous,
But dear for Her cherishing to this beloved and this rocky land.
Over above all the world there, in a tired glory swerved there –
To a fall, the tree that for long had watched Wales glow strong,
Seen Severn, and farm, and Brecon, Black Mountains times without
      reckon.

And tomorrow would be fuel for the bright kitchen – for brown tea,
      against cold night.

Prelude

Will you not give me, June,
Before I go in
To music, with my fingers
A new thing of tune
To win?
(Out of earth remembered to win?)
You have no gifts
Past my worth to make free.
The wind, my hair lifts, – (the love in mind lingers.)
The grass my feet lightly
Treads – will not suffer
Discourtesy.
Give me some truth
Of the wide sight of valley
Severn, fore–Severn, far–Severn and high Wales
For a poet – his ruth.
A tune for the reflection
Of spinney and water sally,
Valley and plain – and the mountainous far region.
Make me sure
I that am pure

With laving water my light-free body.
Make me certain
That had for curtain
But three days gone – ~~the~~ /midnight/ beeches, steady, star steady.
Give me a long
Thread of clear song
That shall tell all
The truth that my heart
Sees ~~clear~~ /so/ to hurt smart.
Call wonder from the deeps
Where poetry hides and sleeps.
What you deny be sure Cotswold shall guilty you hold.
And the winds shall accuse
When I am back in the room.
With pen and paper,
The piano, and wrapping half gloom.
The stars shall accuse you
In the kitchen where
I shall read Shakespeare and labour
At my rough notes
Taken by cottages and sheep cotes.
Dare not the stars –
They are higher than the white scars
And the tops of your trees.
They have seen your beeches
Go under many years.
Many times, and be drawn with rough wooden cars
Over the ways of Autumn where I have kicked leaves,
And in January,
The mist resolves in water drops and grieves.
In mornings of quick goings.
Or nights walking fearlessly.
Give me June out of unbelievable –
But by me known truly –
All you are able
Of your inevitable

Ordered beauty to set down in ink without folly;
Truly told truth of your many, many
Delights of treed hill.
There are not many children of /all/ your family
Have friended Orion
Or by Twyver gone.
My faithfulness you should reward as a courage alone.
With especial riches,
Since truth has right, and there is duty between Cotswold's self and
        man,
Such good as this is.

Ballad for honour

Three things or four
God will not have despised.
The honour of steel and song,
A womans honour.
The honour of air and earth and water.
His Justice on those who deny
Honour to those who watched Sirius glory the sky:
On the white road high above Severn Wales' daughter.
After continual – a days honour of – equity.

And if the singer have a noble wound,
And if his steel were bright,
Where, others, meaner, took comfort and delight.
And if his kiss were clear love,
And his caresses
Of a hand by October browned.
Yet men not honour –
His anger shall find them somewhere.

And if his air were Severn and Wales of mixture,
Of limestone crumbled, and brown soft earth of texture
His earth: and water running down tenderly from

Strange founts under woods or camps
Where the trefoils small lamps
And the first violet makes soft wonder unknown.
His love shall rebuke the meanness of souls not loving –
Removing – with equal justice removing.

And truth as clear as a girls truth,
A night walker.

Courage of a clean heart boy
With the beeches talker,
~~Nodding looking up to the Seven Stars or Capella high.~~

But praise of Cities and noble stone His love,
Gratitude for passed builders, and steady worshippers.
Who loved the sun and friends and song, and so made
Faithfulness to so high a trade.
Building nobly high Peters and Tewkesburys Abbeys,
Damming Twyver, Chelt,
Or Avons small waterways –
God's House of worship towering high above one years thought or
Anything but long devotion of lit candle–night hour
And the watching of other stone, other Abbeys with devotion.

If such he be – what wrong they do who not honour
His life with civic manner
Of respect, and talk grateful of his work got hard
Of the inner word?

Who has praised (not war) but the honour of steel and courage –
Endurance, and friendliness in the worst of distress.
Not killing, but talking; not dying, but living a friend.
Obeying orders and taking Duty out to true end.
Song making and verse making in bitter winters trenches,
Where the tread squenches and the frozen sinews shaking.

Elizabethans who has praised as those friends, his Masters.
Not to /be/ feared but to be

~~The~~ Midnight companions, and ~~the~~ /of/ all love outlasters,
Past Greece or Rome – or France – She.

Towns and the Civic honour and love of streets,
Houses set by houses – of history past all thoughts,
Brought love of centuries to all men, in verse's delights.
Craft and love equal – in the loving use of crafts.

Or Rome – Her ancient honour caught the true
Spirit; not conqueror and invader making way through;
Asia, Cilicia, Egypt, Cappadocia or Lycaonia;
But giving arts and crafts to Vermand and Tours
Beauty to ~~Lyons~~ Clermont, order to Namur, or Nassau,
A better ploughing to the lands of Picardy,
Or Saintonge – or slopes of Cotswold watching Severn Sea.
New metal, new words in order like great ceremony,
And dignity of usage worthy of Europe Her Age.

For honour a ballad – if men honour not such a one –
Let them deny the sun.
~~And~~ Sword, verse, and song – these put aside a common thing,
Let them not war or sing.
And leave honour, walk night never, with truth have done
Till God with pity compel all –
They repentance tell all –
And keep tears till there happen some reverence
For what from God came hence –
Spirit of soldier and singer, and night's priest of worship,
Remembering the Western joy, ~~and~~ the frost pain of France.

For to his honour / high / stone is raised; therein
Kings ~~and~~ have right and soldiers and great makers.
Priests serve them, Counsellors with words men shakers –
Making – And merchants, sailors, and civic folk;
Ceremonial observance raising the mind from common chance.
Noble words guarding thought safe from mean saying or poetrys sin.

Not in those Houses may the not honourers go –

Soldier and poet lightly reckoned, God is /made/ naught
And will not take their worship, or their presence know,
Why in His House to worship, ~~what~~ these deniers of him,
These pale of spirit watch white stone and coloured windows dim,
Words of set wonderful old beauty to repeat
Whose reputation is but of the home room or the common street.

God cannot accept what truth will not accept of men,
His Spirit is first truth, then reverence, then worship.
(The day – the half day – and the high night star lit.
Who knows them not has no honour, must learn his lot)
~~Who lets these slip –~~
In sin is so far that the new birth is to be humbly entreated for.)

Song

Dresses and movement and a clear blood known
By Whitehall or Regent Street –
Even the night walker on Chilterns or Cotswolds alone,
Must love, feel his heart beat.

Though a soldiers honour he has, and of singer thereto –
With pride like any young girls high.
Loving Rome, a boat sailer, great verse, and late night through;
He salutes and goes nobler by.

London Bridge

Borrow stood there, but I remembered not him,
But Carlyle being brought out from useless work in the night dim;
To watch the gray river , the gulls, and long
For tea, my delight – which for once should be hot and strong.
Of Borrow thought, but more of weariness,
And tea, and the first train, and work to redress
My candle light failure – and rest my mind with making.

The gray light grew coloured – there was less and less
Of night – I thought of Marryat and of Fielding ill.
While Thames slid under to London, and to Chiswick Mall.

London Bridge

The nearly dying evening stirred in light
Only in the dark waters and barge files –
All else was quiet, save the quarters chime all quiet.
Poetry was for the having, but tired, tired was I –
Truth and beauty from me, with Cold Storage to work at;
Money to get, and all cloudy wonder high in the sky.
August gloomed; there was little of harvest month
Or any month to see by Southwark or City –
Time was tired – hours slid on without reckoning or date;
Music, verse reading; ... all good for me little Time heeding,
Hard work like fire to earn money so later I might write.
Proud of the job, too often beaten for my deep heart's bleeding.
Which should be crying to God against his gift and such fate
As no writer earning as soldier work chance for ever
Should have come to – Pauls knew my tale and watched
              Thames-gate –
Whom I had praised in music worthy of Wren's endeavour.

Of Death

I thought, if one of those threatening shells catches me,
/Catches/ Me, as it must each minute, such anger, such danger, –
(Certain to hit) I must lose my chance of music –
No more ~~for me~~ the great hope of saying music out – /(and that hurts
              me)/
Which earth meant me for, and Cotswold in the coppice thick.
(Certain to hit, certain. I must smoke. I <u>must</u> smoke.) Then
The strafe passed, I must go message running, or mending again,

Down the trench, Bach filling my heart with pain
For beauty, I'd walk swift ridding my heart out of fear.
~~And~~ Lucky to be moving the others shaken and to stay still there.
Lucky to move. Gloucester were all immortal I
Thought and turned to wonder at their courtesy,
Courage and goodness in the long march and unborne strain,
Cotswold children, born of limestone and washed earth sun and rain.
Only – they'd not as I /would/ be, a maker again –
Being nightwalker, long ago, earth and the stars had celebrated
Consecration for me – and the night ways me awaited
To bless the walker who loved Portway to leave
His bed as quiet as dream folk not to awaken –
Not to stir parents (his loved father) by door shaken,
To creep down stairs with Cranham Corner steady in his mind,
Boots softly on; not a sound – then free walking with heart talking –
The stars above were better than soft bed to grieve.
(Those Gloucesters kept their beds and had sleepy heads.
Shameful ~~and~~ save those who tilled lands, or ploughed round heads,
Or used all body.) Death thought there as a change –
But God would let me, ere the spirit out of body range –
Write my thoughts, would he not, and pay the hard lot
Of bother, father had to give me music's chance.
(They played pandar to the devil with electricity's evil)
And ~~hearer~~ here I was, ~~as my~~ /a soldier, now,/ fearing little, in
               France.
(Nothing of death, only to make music, not to lose that.)
Death at Laventie was a shell hitting middle from body.
At Richebourg the thing at shaving made my hand unsteady.
(Three feet off, the shell; and then perhaps just as well.)
At Tilleloy the matter of the greatest of songs all of men
Of ending, and there was a poem of Aveluy again
That said a thing of death .... But five miles off I stuck
In Death's Valley, thigh deep, far too tired to curse my luck.
But never pain there wished me ever to die.
In Grandcourt – through a raid slept a sheet over my head.
Standing, and Ypres gassed me, and dented my helmet.

Tilleloy tore my coat – and Vermand a sick heart
Weak body lying bored under the German wires –
Their bullets and our bullets and bare misses in scores.
(That was near Death. I thought my music had gone.
But reckoned to write with one hand. Round cursing I spun
To damn and curse, and black damn black curse the spite
That got me danger of arm, and holed my right.
But could not get me Blighty for all my near death plight.)
Death – I saw Death at Rouen in the tawny rock.
Rocked with delight at October Tilleloy's dawns high.
Took Death by threefold fear in the place of battery,
Ypres cannon set shoulder by shoulder for great shock.
Body from soul bursting but for the soul.
Death? Bach drew me out of such fear; Whitman,
Beethoven's deep soul triumphing above far Orion
Funk was a fear of losing my work chance here.
And since the 2/5 were born gentlemen – scorn
Put aside, as Cotswold, talk of Death's end, or portal,
They had ploughed earth, I sailed boat, we were all immortal.

Humility – and Her friend

Some men have found God, and proclaimed God –
But they were not of Cotswold where the road in turf
Runs noble to the northward over edge of earth.
~~But they were not night walkers.~~
Not nightwalkers they were, under Regulus or the Bear.
But (sacred minded – with clear body) I have found Rome,
Her spirit touched me – and in some way of April's mood
Shakespeare called me outwards to draw resistless home.
Bridges by the Cranham beeches, Davies by small Priding wood.
Bach in that room of firelight drew immortality home.
Virgil Englished, Whitman set clear to music, some
Violin etching of a curve of dream – when no
Hindrance troubled, and it might come over to snow.

Surely the days would bring me to my heart's power?

But she would take all demands with quiet heart,
Hoping with prayer for me, supporting injury
Nuisance and noise, with no more than the clear refusal
To give a kiss for Bach played Cotswold-well –
Her God-Creator omnipotens, but to answer prayers.
Give me such chance for such gifts her affection could tell.

The Far Horns

Beethoven sounded them often and often,
They are the soul of Keats enwrapped with earth
(Autumn loving) The call of them gave birth
(One September dusk light) to a Stratford pair,
Whose son is praised against India or the East Empire.
They sound a mellow third in a chestnut wood
And of pines – by Side or Penn I have known of them.
Suddenly calling so
The heart to know
Beyond our first mind lies the all searchéd place,
That Merville had for one space.
Or Varennes knew
When for a winters honour divine Orion
Triumphed, never again so.
But best the stubble under Dryhill where the scabious
Keeps some imperious
Memory of Rome.
But trefoil talks Her deep heart on the sheep walks.
A golden thing ~~like a long note~~ /sung/ on a violin string
Of thought – a far pipe
Farther
Than the far horns;
Listening
One would love it, rather.

Love

After so mixed a night of work delight
And walking under the
Stars, parting asunder the
Hawthorn branches.
Winter stanches
The hidden sap.
To return (to Eridanus ~~with~~ /my/ eyes up)
Tea, the Notebook, Carlyle
The Long Island book,
And Quartetts pages filling in with black lines.
Turning to verse at times;
When in the dawn's surprise
Faintly whitening skies
Over Cotswold to make the east soon show bold –
With the faint stirs
Of the unimagined airs
Faint unimagined music
Breathed in my mind
Of how one sick
Kept kind, so I might have way
Of working, and no
Reward save her hearts glow,
For no thanks is
Expected of apprentices,
Though anothers blood flow.
I'd walk the brick bridge and a few yards further
Thinking, "Light to gather,
And she not see it,
Early Winter to miss.
Virgil's light, Thoreau's light.
A night's working, with no reward of a kiss.
It would have seemed
Not worth while before Riez Bailleul –
Dawn's truth lit,
Dryhill slope grew azure and dreamed.

At the time

We'd ache with hunger, cold, and bitterness of spirit
That a Command put on, men near over done –
When the mud, and strain had lessened, we'd get again
Orders to dig a ditch – or to be harried, and to bear it.

We'd hope with such hot longing for the love of friends.
Tired out, with dull longing – but looking for amends;
Amends in the after time – with books, music till the ends
Of dawn, the clear light drove to think – Ypres, and St Julien's.

We'd march a day – and dig (hell's risk) at midnight –
They expected letters interesting with no names –
And all the news cut out; and as for poems
Who would print such, if the hour were given of joy or delight.

~~They~~ Never was happiness so needed of men, – the time
After the dark was tea and letters, ~~and~~ rest of night's ~~ake~~ ache
They got the poems, which cost craft, and life risk – for the sake
Of spirit there driving; and small hope of right fame having.
Who got the poems – for thanks, sin like Hell's lost, and are not sick.

A bit from my "Gloucestershire Rhapsody"

The trees talked it, and horses, went trampling by.
There is no end to glory when blood is high,
And we that are Gloucester's own, since She has gracious grown
Will take a day of April as it is meant in mind.

Cotswold called an infinite love from the deeps
Of Her – Severn remembered the galley sweeps;
Thought Dane – as Cotswold Roman – and lifted Her whole
Soul to the day; all the history and gossip keeps
She heard in twenty centuries of change, and strange people.

March with Her wind, which might be great, is kept friend;

For one day man is allowed equality, and /of/ godlike mind
Comrade with March and Cotswold – Severn broadening all-grand.

All love from all memory called out – Beethoven, Belloc;
The Lament Song – and watching the scarred hills, "Puck
of Pooks Hill" – and my own music surging up and up.

Happy is he, Ulysses

By the gold light he works of the shaded lamp,
Writes, turns Ben Jonson over, and walks out to see
Distant Cotswold, with its cottage and high camp.
One minute, then to Quartett again, so carefully
You might think Carlyle or Stanford stood by his shoulder;
When leaving that man of Westminster and gray Galloway,
That great gentleman's book – he grows bolder and bolder,
Writes surely, with a blue smoke of tobacco puffing,
Drinks tea, and sees the thoughts line go onward free.
(Thank God, a truth of earth; clean thinking, no stuffing.)
Takes praise to himself – and has the master's long paid satisfaction.
Reads "Chambers Encyclopedia" or revives thought
Of how Goethe or Whitman or great Samuel wrought –
Returning – with deep musing – under stars his dim eyes
Could not see fair – by Bolt Court or Gough Square there.
Walks out again toward the little bridge of Longford –
And thinks "I have come home, and Laventie is answered –
The cold of Chaulnes paid, and long nights of Ypres on guard.
Earth chose me – pain has paid for me – I shall have reward".

Southwark

As dun at night as any manufacturing
Town, where the writers dug a garden and heard sing
Blackbird, expecting rain, or after light rain –

But there is one square, and Thames, by the ugly bridge.
Thames Street, where I worked a week of Cold Storage,
The last muscle using of my soldiers body:
Till a hurt came, keeping steady, for work all ready.
With a thought of playwrights great in a golden age,
I have walked there as elsewhere of all London Town,
The one of masters following, the one through seeing
Truth of the formal page, and strict form of Morley.
Who saw stars also and had their shutters thrown.
February, June October November with the embers
Of the nights fire still waking on the hearthstone.
But Shes a draggled Borough after the eaved
Timber and brick of Fifteen ninety or sixteen hundred,
Little wonder the night walker with clear eyes grieved
To see so little of pride. Present so far sundered
From past, when stone was raised so that men believed,
And served God better than now, when mean brick and mortar
Stands for a Church; that
Drayton nor Daniel had dared say one word, nor blundered.

The Elements

A writer thought "How lovely to rise and lave
My smooth fair body with water clear from earth drawn.
Ponder on it, and dig the garden, so little garden.
Drink tea, and smoke. Write, thanking my Aunts kindness
(Hoping to return work chance and all, as doubtless
I did – a friend of mine, and beyond thought kind,
Often ....) It was a chance of work past my hopes, save she
Would force tea, and trap to food, so it was terror to me.
So I'd go walking by Cotswold streams set a-talking
By a short course and steep from hills azure, green,
Through the hawthorn hedges, and orchards dimly seen.
There by Haw Bridge, and Forthampton, and the hill whose name
Is gone from me – where the silver brook earth bore and laughed silver,

By the landslide to Hartpury, Maisemore and so where I came.
(To see Great Peters like Leonora over ~~the~~ Severn meadows)
To talk and work, returning courtesy with company.
Till she'd go upstairs; then no more talking, in lamp shadows
Golden and black on gold, I'd work hours untold
Reading Goethe and Shakespeare, seeing Longford meadows.
And getting notes on paper, and verse square bold,
Till the day star died out over Kingsholm, and light soaked up gloom,
Quartetts and tea, tobacco, Elizabethans – none better of those.
My Aunt would come down fresh cheeked for all her years,
To find me writing, and I'd smile and talk my thanks,
Lie down, covered with a rug for one hour, with eyes clear as on high
        Cotswold then.

All Souls Day

The poplars by the breathing road
Were coloured by bright fallen streaks
Of ~~colour~~ /lit leaves/ that the Autumn breaks,
Or chooses one by one; the strewed
Path of mourners for dead soldiers' sakes.

Dark dressed, moving by alight poplars,
With all the worship North French faces
Have (in their estaminet or home places
Lit) Robecq folk came to the years-
Of-ceremony – the ages' grief of losses.

Tolled monotonously the long bell – slow
With comrade sound to the soft air,
Touching the cheek with frost, and clear,
Mourning blue clad and noble Poilus
Another earth had taken, that this bore.

Mary, they called for Comforters
Christ, nightwalker, caller of men,

God, the Unknown, Who had let down
(As no human) this black distress
On Europe, Robecq had sorrowed again.

Earth wept with them, of this blood, Her's,
What, of so much pain, so long a service,
To be given but safety a common grace;
And for loving labour, a thought of tears?
"Creator omnipotens, pity us, earth and us!)

In the billets, or dismissed, strolling
Gloucesters that had of their own earth, spirit,
Watched them, thinking, "We too may inherit
Such a lamenting, such a bell, calling;
Who hoped for Gloucester and calm lives near it."

"If they, so we – but poor ~~French~~ mothers.
We have seen them – those brave ones of blue,
Noble helmeted" – The bell called through
All thought, of all earth – of brothers
To these – it seemed; Europe's old woe.

The Great Gentleman

Dekker turned back to Heywood
"Hear master Ben boasting!
Thought of Cataline or no Cataline,
This takes some besting."

"Is there not Antony to
Our need and guidance?
Have we not Tamburlaine still,
And Du Bellay's Angevin France."

Great gentleman Ben turned
"You say well – Ulysses desired
Little after long wanderings to see
But blue smoke upspired."

"But these folks will /not/ give to me
Even wanderers reward.
Who in Flanders kept my art
Bright and my sword."

"Du Bellay had friendship
Denied not preeminence –
Marguerite cared for him.
Fellows praised him, his lovely sense."

"Take wine friends, Burning Pestle
And "Roaring Girl"
We'll see Pauls white in the morning
And Ludgate Hill."

"Before this thought not drown
In ruddy full wine.
~~Greet~~ Curse theatre goers
They are not of masters discoverers.
Your chance like mine."

Ely

Passed in a minute or so in a moving train,
A wonder on meadows, a lovely Abbey in a plain
Of river, and drained marsh; and sunlight golden all through.
A boy, loving Gloucester, seeing a new thing and secretly envying.
(What! was this new wonder his loved one to outdo?)
Watched and wondered, and kept his thoughts silent so
He should not say right praise.
                    After from a writer
Praising Normans so never they had praise the greater.
She was better known, the memory staying and of verse creator.
One of French blood stirred to glorify English mood –
Flooding his words in order with divine foreordained
Natural power, out to prose liked the never gained

Music of October – battering midnight Cotswold high in the wood.
Ely was known a wonder, and the lover of our town
Was cast down:
(A little) until he saw once again high Peter's draw
Soul and mind and flesh to his great power
In a March hour.
And friended Ely – was afraid nor to lie no more.
What shall guard spirit but white stone with age gone mellow?

Song

Past my window dawn and down.
Through the open shutters thrown
Pass the birds the first awaking
And the light wind peace breaking.

Now the ink will dry on pen –
And the paper take no more
Thoughts of beauty from the far
Night, or remembered day of men.
Cotswold breaking the dark or standing
Brave as the sun, with white scar.

Now my footsteps shall go light
By the fence and bridge till white
The farm show, that till now had glimmered
In the trees July had summered.

To a friend

Who was born of Gloucester earth
And for pride of Englands truth,
Made him soldier,
For wise none bolder.

Who was sweet when others sad –
Kept his pack on shoulders, had
Cotswold about them.
Songs would shout them.

It was he that kept good temper
When the breaking point of hamper,
Weight and tired being
Made others quarrelling

It was he who praised my book.
And thanked me with a lovely look
Pleased with love of friends
To the death's end.

It was he who reproached me so
For taking Machine gun job although
There was a dug out
For getting writing out.

And in Ypres haze I watched them,
Safe and trembling, how it smashed them. –
When the Gloucesters went
And I sentry behind.

Watching high above the battle,
Dazed and trembling with the rattle,
Glad not to go over.
(Sorry not to be there.)

September Ypres had a mist
Azure hid the shell that missed
Or that which hit him.
And laid still dead him.

Whether Gloucester buried Gloucester
I know not, my job was watcher.
To dodge shrapnel, see,
What to aim at, might be.

Elizabethans

Shakespeare was my friend (feared) at sixteen years.
Johnson "the Alchemist" at twenty two or so.
Beaumont and Fletcher, Marlowe next my gain –
Puzzled making out the reputation of a masters show.
And never finding it, and never finding it.
There was "Roaring Girl" and of "the Golden West["]
But not till London was made manifest
In one short summer the fat works of Ben Jonson,
Half a crown, and Morley half a crown.
Then I knew delight, then masters in the late night
I had, new pride, and Beethoven put aside –
For Marston, Shirley, Greene, and Ford my delight.
Who'd feed my fill, and go to muse on them
By Westminster or stray lanes of City by Thames –
(Knowing why my blood held of /life/ such ~~life~~ high mood,
Knowing why makers kept watch of high star acres;
And why the unresting spirit to me was good.)
Putting aside the greatest of song with gladness,
For the strong manliness of the Great Company of playwriters.
Who had their job, and took delight, deep till midnight.
Verse of clear wonder, out of earth love brought to arts-right.

The Poets of my County

One was a happy serious boy in lands
Of meadows – and went to France, and kept his hands
For bayonet readier than the pen, being likely
To dream into a poem, men should not ever see.
And one was sailor by Horn and Valparaiso, wrote
Such tale of Pompey as showed him rightly the great.
Another, the first, of St Thomas wrote imagining,
Of whom cuckoo flowers ~~made~~ brought/ immortal lines, and did sing
Like water of clear water – like April's spirit of Spring.

But what of Taylor, water-poet, who left desiring
The Roman town for the rich one, fame his heart so firing
He'd not heave cargoes nor draw wages by Severn.
And one wrote worthy verses indeed of the Four ways,
Coming in, watched of high clouds, for commercial days,
And military: another saw Ryton and wrote so –
Another yet wrote sonnets none so fool should forget.
(Of Rupert Brooke – gold winter on the sheets
Where light made memory of history of that room's happenings.)
The love of Edward Thomas is nightwalkers promise.
But I praised Gloucester City as never before – and lay
By Tilleloy keeping spirit in soul with the way
Coopers comes over from Eastward sees Rome all the way.
But none have helped me. Deep to Hell Gloucester let betray me.
Pain no word can say of me. Hell has racked me, and God not helped
        me.

Portrait of a Coward

True he'd have fought to death if the Germans came –
But an hours battering after a days battering
Brought his soul down to quivering, with small shame.
And he was fit to run, if his chance had come.
But Gloucesters of more sterner frame and spirit
Kept him in place with/out/ reproach, (sweet blood inherit
From hills, and nature) said no word and kept him there.
True, he'd have fought to death, but Laventie's needing
Was a nerve to hide the pain of the soul bleeding –
Say nothing, and nothing ever of God to beg.
He hurt more, did fatigues, and was friend to share
What food was not his need; of enemies not heeding.
Everybody was glad – (but determined to hide the bad)
When he took courage at wiremending and shot his leg,
And got to Blighty, no man saying word of denying.

Cry of the People

Historians, poets, why do you exalt battles?
And write coloured stories of flag and steel,
We pay the prices, who love God, and dear earth that till
Is not the poet, the priest, to be honoured the greatest –
We have heard David of Israel his words, and know –
Honour of soldier and singer – but far too often
Europe has suffered pain from your tales of contest,
We have dug the coins and old swords for battle were wroughten.
Our life should be earth and calm living and the evening free,
Why should we bear an agony false history brings on the folk – ?
If base statesmen and cruel soldiers bring down the yoke,
You helped to make, Tell truth, make our lives loved who see
No hope in peace, till you say what your hearts peace does talk.

Of the Sea

Cornwall surges round Zennor like the true delight
Of earth all savage with a force enemy to man –
Bude streams a long roller of curled gathering foam.
But nothing more than Masefield I have come truly
To know, Great ocean with huge strength untamed or stilly,
Or Marryat's sea affairs so local and snug of the focs'le.
Mightiness of the wide Atlantic hiding its strength,
Or tempested Long Island or Massachussetts land
Bretagne, and Baltic, the Californian long sand length;
The dark October lowering of South Dorset
"Dynasts" has shown to me, these are not to forget –
Seen of my deep mind reading the northeast blind
Dawn through. But of all things most of the sea to me –
There is Longney Reach to Priding beating victoriously
In a great June exultation of half-tide Severn.
And Trafalgars ships moving like painted things
Over a painted sea – and Walt Whitmans true sight, haunted sea.

"The perfume, the faint creaking of the cordage – melancholy
Rhythm –" and this is ocean's poem to compel
Poetry in the heart of a boy late /night/ working:
Men giving life of the huge unseen mid Atlantic swell.

War books

What did they expect of our toil and extreme
Hunger – the perfect drawing of a hearts dream?
Did they look for a book of wrought art's perfection,
Who promised no reading, nor praise, nor publication?
Out of the heart's sickness the spirit wrote.
For delight, or to escape hunger, or of war's worst anger.
When the guns died to silence, and men would gather sense
Somehow together, and find this was life indeed.
And praise another's nobleness, or to Cotswold get hence.
There we wrote – Corbie Ridge – or in Gonnehem at rest.
Or Fauquissart or worlds death songs ever the best.
One made sorrows praise passing the church where silence
Opened for the long quivering strokes of the bell –
Another wrote all soldiers praise, and of France and night's stars –
Served his guns, got immortality, and died well.
But Ypres played another trick with its danger on me,
Kept still the needing and loving of action body;
Gave no candles, and nearly killed me twice as well.
And no souvenirs though I risked my life in the stuck Tanks.
Yet there was praise of Ypres, love came sweet in hospital –
And old Flanders went under to ~~the~~ long ~~loved~~ ages of plough
　　　　　thought in my pages.

Sounds   After E Thomas

Dear to the heart
Violin and piano sound a note apart,
The heart
Catches them, one alone on the high hills
And happy is known.
One note
Out of the limestone or rot
Of leaves,
When Autumn grieves –
The chalk,
Or tranquil meadows where the Abbey shows.
Out of these comes
The one note of Romance.
The single
Tone which sounds ~~a long~~ alone
The true secret
The heart's thought with nothing does /ever/ mingle.
Gloucester sounds third,
Chilterns has a word
Of Midland truth
In her beech woods smooth
Of trunk, leaves yet unstirred.
And on the brown
Pastures or wasted meadows
By Merville town,
The lit and gracious
Whiteness of October's
Tower
Shows to be known
Wonder for more than an hour.
By Side and Slad
Music is to be had.
Sussex not denied
Truth of sounds beauty

From truths eyes
Known and had surely.
Beethoven
Touches one
String of his sixteen
And the whole sorrow of man
Is, from time it has been.
Stars and hurt
Of the keen smart
Of beauty – or past comfort
Pain.
And Brahms makes stubble
An alive trouble
To the mind
As in September
It is golden and kind.
Bach does all
Of a mortal.
Schumann weeps like a child
Heart undefiled
On his wife's breast,
Or wanders the happiest
Of lone mortals under another-world pines.
Great sorrow
Mans sorrow,
And earths hope for morrow
That the soul divines
In vain –
It never comes;
He must write his cheated heart out in nights glooms.
These of the masters,
The learnt and able
Building shapers
Of sound to noble
And approved makings –
To the worlds wonders

Adding new things.
Master works and of ages, cares.
Yet the single things
Hold us, there clings
Beauty more to the sudden
Girls song in Spring
Heard from some sudden
Leafy covering.
And rough romance
From the lit blinds,
When "Spanish Sailors"
or "Tarry Trowsers" sounds.
(That dear thing of /to/ minds
From the resting fallows
Or the ploughing grounds
Come
Dear to their hearts as Earth's scents
In Autumn ....)
A solitary tune
Heard of the walker
In June
Or in October
When the year is sober
And leaves fall
And the croon
Of winds rises slowly
To the great wholly-
Glorious battle of dry winds
Clouds hiding the moon.
Then the walker shouts
Out his delights
Great joy taken alone.
This music itself –
Body joy and spirit
Together known.
And there are no single

Nor third sounds
But the great orchestra
Blasting full brass and drum tones,
Strings, wind, and kettle drums,
Strings pulling great passion from
Their wood and fibre.
To the Ninth, Neighbour,
And C Minor Symphony,
(Hamburg and Vienna)
The "Sea" and B Eroica
As if by Tiber
The waves were white
Cassius with Caesar
Daring the white
Foam.
Or I a boy
Walking Cotswold high.
They brave, I braver.
They dead, I aliver
Than the rocking trees
In great blastings of seas
Of sound like St Ives
Or the Orkneys.
I alone, I alone –
With the glimpsed moon,
And nothing, nothing
Else save the Romans
Passed, but my friends
In the woods or the lonely
Commons ends.
Knowing Immortality, daring October.
Cotswold given to my hands.

THE BOOK OF FIVE MAKINGS

<u>First poem</u>:

O what will you turn out, book, to be?
Who are not my joy, but my escape from the worst
and most accurst of my woe? Shall you be poetry,
Or tell truth, or be of past things the tale rehearsed?

<u>"The book of Five makings"</u>.

Feb 1925.

(in texture)

<u>Ivor Gurney</u>.

Detail of title page

First poem

O what will you turn out, book, to be?
Who are not my joy, but my escape from the worst
And most accurst of my woe? Shall you be poetry,
Or tell truth, or be of past things the tale rehearsed?

Thoughts

Watching books open before me in my daze of pain –
Chaucer, Ballads, "Leaves of Grass["], and "Voces Intimae",
Still numbed with torture, never a real let in pain ....
Yet keeping faith – the black wrong London day by day does against
        me.
Who have great honour's right, to ask without any denying; –
See there is Petit de Julleville, and Mozarts Quartetts;
Robert Bridges (in strange binding repels and hurts)
Most honoured; Shakespeare /master/ of all free writing company.
(O Ballads, which open to a clang of words like soldier iron)
But pain weighs so heavy on all the sense of my days –
It is an effort to read even Francis Jammes with heed, –
Chaucer is an antiquarian, mind-remembered praise......

I who in Line, lousy, worried with deaths and dirts
Aeschylus, Keats and Ronsard stretched in signaller wise;
Get no more good of scholarship than moment's pain defying;
Love, honour, companionship, taken from me and gone....
And the City has done this, London, to honour bound inevitably;
(Once golden) forgets all shame in Her black sins day by day done.

Thoughts

Watching the books before me in my /dazed/ pain,
Chaucer and Ballads, "Leaves of Grass", "Voces Intimae" –
Dazed with torture /still,/ with never a real let in pain, –
I know the black wrong London eternally plots against me –
Who have right of Her great honour, and to ask without denying.
See, there is Petit de Julleville, and Mozart's Quartetts,
Robert Bridges (in a queer /black/ binding /that/ repels and hurts)
Most honoured, and Shakespeare master of free heart /writing/ all
   poet's Company.
(The Ballads, which opened, give a clang out like /great/ iron.)
But all the torture weighs so heavy on /all/ my days,
It is an effort to read even Francis Jammes with heed –
Chaucer is an almost false and mind-supported praise.
I who in the Line read, /(lousy)/ worried with deaths and dirts,
Aeschylus, Keats and Ronsard stretched /lazy/ in signaller wise, –
Get no more good of scholarship than an anguish defying
All love, all glory, all hope of making my /true/ own;
And the City has done this, to most honour is /being/ bound
   inevitably ....
/London;/ It is London - the old golden City; it is the Hell called
  London.

October in Exile

Blasting great guns like my own wind and midnight trees,
Robecq, near Toussaints time, flared with a windy sunset,
Magnificent, untamed; clear light over ~~fros~~ storming leas,
Of Flanders – I stood to watch this, in orchard of billet.
Glory! It gave one hope again to walk body three hours
At midnight, to Cranham, past bare roads and blasting beeches.
To return clear blooded to the warm room where ardour met
Tea and tobacco, candles, Shakespeare's swifter pages
(After the storm) set up over paper and ink-pot.
Gloucesters smothered regrets in cards, I could not:
Being full of actualities and wonderful images.
Nor forget beloved makings, nor strict Carlyle's high powers,
Holding the strength to working till one dawnlight sees.
(London or Cotswold) knowing one's strength the nobler
For labour; others shamefully asleep in useless bed.
Working, wrestling night through, after fury of walking /that/
Desired ten miles of Cotswold, readying power for the ways
Of any /way/ getting work done, imagination hot or not so hot.
Robecq, you brought many things – This tale is one of those.

October in Exile

Blasting great guns like my own wind and [deletion] /dusky/ trees,
Robecq, at about Toussaints time, with a flaring sunset
Magnificent, untamed; at last clear light over /storm-tossing/ leas
Of Flanders – watching this in the orchard, a way from the billet;
/(Rapt)/ It gave one hope again to walk hard three /hot/ hours
At midnight, to Cranham, past bare roads and blasting beeches,
And return clear blooded to the lit room/, warm,/ where ardour met
Tea and tobacco, music paper, and Shakespeare's /clear/ swift pages
Set for a guide over the blackening paper and ink-pot.
Gloucesters played cards past dreams, but I could not
Rid my heart of these wonderful and loved /night/ images –
Nor forget Northern makings nor strict Carlyle's powers;
Which hold the strength till breaking till one dawn sees,
Coming up over Cotswold, and knows one /grown/ nobler
For labouring, (others asleep in most shameful bed)
/Working,/ Wrestling the night through after /hot/ walking that
Desired 10 miles of Cotswold   readying power for the ways
/(Any)/ Of getting work from an imagination for accomplishment
        too hot.

Elizabethans

Past men writing long, drawing the curtain of dawn,
Holding strength well with digging or with warehouse working,
Trusting to gods' honour their manuscripts for the praise
Of later generations; happy in midnight's most frank talking.
Love of comrades, praise of craftsmen equal in reckon.
Generous whatever Marston, Heywood, Dekker had done;
Now in another place to shrink with unmastered loathing
From this time-politeness ever above sanctity known.
Well dressed-ness /set/ above any honour of creation.
(O Male-things immaculate by Knightsbridge or Mayfair ways!)
Who have no thought of Shirley or greatest Jonson
(Holding ignorant the mind from even "The Alchemist" in scorn)
How friends of Mermaid, Phoenix, swordsmen, navvies of making –
Had shuddered to think of such evil corruption of the Old Town –
The Old City that once to /a/ world, an age, for brave and golden,
But sins now even without joy or the true sinner's reckoning
And boasts no longer of great work from sundown till sundown.

Elizabethans

Elizabethans writing their great works out till /curtain of/ dawn –
And holding the strength with digging and with warehouse working;
Trusting their manuscripts would be somehow kept for the praise
Of later generations; and glorying in midnight talking,
Loving of comrades, and craftsmen /of/ equal reckon
Of what Marston or Heywood, or another had last /masterly/ done –
How they would have shrunk with terror and with strong loathing
From a /bare/ time which has politeness for its sanctity known;
And cleanliness a virtue past praise of /any/ creation –
(Immaculately dressed slim male creatures by Knightsbridge ways
Or Clapham's) never having heard much /talk/ of great Jonson –
(Of "The Alchemist," Ignorant of "Cataline" in /light-mind/ scorn)
They had shuddered to think their free greatness of man's making –
Should come to the judgement /in centuries/ of such feeble London;
Which prefers anything to truth, sins black without /joy or/ sinners
　　　reckoning.

From Laventie Line

There were not many escapes from Laventie Line –
(Few troops there, we needed whenever called)
Laventie, La Gorgues, Estaires, Merville and Rouge Croix;
Escapes from the summer's misery, Winter's Hell of cold:
(But the finest of all places in Autumn was small Robecq.)
(The dearest place) Robecq - and after that unvext
Estaires, where papers sold, clean town and humanly old.
Merville glimmering white in the distance of June ....
Tower of memory .... Dear and all-desired for the lack
Of Cotswold villages, ways on hill-side, so sudden
Full of Cotswold to the plain of river, whether of summer or in flood;
But things turned so, La Gorgues chiefly was our civic dwelling.
Laventie with exact plane-trees; hurt and still fine:
Laventie with its Town air after foolish strain and use of the Line.
At La Gorgues, a mill stood moved by the rivers flooding,
Watching a meadow as of History and battle old.
People were kind – Gold streamed through the roof past telling;
"Le Telegramme", "Le Petit Parisien" at midday came for paying.
This was our pay for soldiering watching Aubers brooding.

So few places we went to

So few places we went to from Laventie Line.
Laventie, La Gorgues, Estaires, Merville and Rouge Croix ....
With one unforgettable staying at Autumn Robecq.
But though the dearest place was that last, and /the/ next
Estaires, where papers sold, clean town and humanly old;
Merville with the church noble, ~~milky~~ /glooming far/ white in June
Of tall tower ... all these we desired; /desired –/ for our desolate lack
Of the Cotswold villages and ways high on hillside, and so sudden
Fall of Cotswold to the plain of meadows, /flooding/ river below.
But since the thing was such; La Gorgues chiefly ~~was~~ our dwelling
~~Was, or~~ /Civil/ Laventie with plane trees, hurt and /to us/ still fine
For its town air, for soldiers tired with the Line's /foolish/ strain.
One small stream, a red /brick/ mill, and a river flowing,
This was all Gloucesters got for their soldiering /hard/ a week.

Like Hebridean

Great sea water surged to its green height of white,
Clamouring in the stone arch, ages on ages all
Had made – Turning at last to seas's natural delight,
Water from the deep playing first its great free game here.
(Zennor Head grim it was, granite of old Cornwall.)
So long the Sea had been toy thing to hearing and sight,
After great poetry music - it was mere relief great
To watch and hear rage of sea water hammering on granite stone here.
So, the Sagas were not lies, Chanties, and certain loved music...
Men had told truth. December in strong despite
Battered with wind and water old County of Cornwall.
(Seagulls uttering drear, flying momently, their strange call.)
Until now ploughland had kept my truth; colour , mystery of ground,
Rise to hide heaven of earth, or sudden white or green fall;
Before this tame thing, Sea, was honoured for all virtue.
Yet now the white uptossing surge, great hoarse-voiced sound,
Compelled admiration – surf in leagues all of elation ....
The Poets were not liars, here also was glory to praised and found.

"Hebridean"

How the green great sea water surged to its /height of/ white
Clamouring in the stone arch ages on ages all
Had made - There was a glory of natural delight.
The Sea for the first time known here playing its /true great/ ~~great~~
          game here.
(/Grim/ Zennor Head it was, granite of old Cornwall.)
After so much disappointment of hearing and /of/ sight,
After ~~great~~ /famed/ sea verse, such tame water, it was / relief and /
          great
To watch and hear the rage of seawater hammering granite stone
          here –
The sagas not lies, nor ~~sea stories, and~~ /Chanties; nor/ certain
          / achieved / music,
Known for truth; December harming /all/ with strong despite ....
(And the white seagulls, their lone /drear/ romantic call.)
At last one might praise Cornwall without / hurt of lying-poetry /
          ~~true shame~~ here...
At last Sea proved of poetry it's magnificence the right.
Zennor Head redeemed what my Gloucester heart greatly had blamed.
And what man had written was not beauty out of pain forgotten.

Salisbury Close

Of Salisbury Close, one might have dreamed in the night
For beauty, and prayed to keep memory of such a fair sight.
So beautiful and wise in grave honour of way.
April beauty on old order to endure infinite
Years it seemed; yet high beauty goes with gravity of Spring
Growing to thought. We, Gloucesters, bitterly at training
On the damned Plain, felt blood at the sight to sing.
(Gloucester remembering standing up all glimmering white)
Glad not to compare, beauty of another Day –
Our own wonderful magic-touched Abbey preferring,
And happy with Constable's, Edward Thomas' delight.
Till it was time go seek out a Restaurant,
And drink civil brown tea at last, the while on musing
Of Borrow hurrying from London, and on Ely and Durham
            magnificent.
How in another month we might be past all fearing
Of beauty taken away, or any hope to make or write;
By one outburst of barrage, or a sniper's choosing.
So drank this tea with true care, remembering lazing
A little before the turn of walking – or the settling to work for the
            night.

Salisbury Close

Salisbury Close is one of the things that one might
Have dreamed, and kept ~~close~~ /strong/ hold /on/ from the gift-
          ~~m~~/t/aking night.
So beautiful and wise in its ~~sort~~ /honour/ of way ....
Of order and April beauty to endure /for/ infinite
Years it seemed; yet to vanish when the Youth of the Spring
Changed to gravity. We, Gloucesters, training in hate (and /hate/
          right)
Our course of useless suffering on the Plain – /in blood/ felt sing
Our hearts in us at this lovely wonder standing up all white –
No need jealousy for Gloucester, this was a different, and a
Not-envied kind of beauty to our own older /birth-given/ Town.
Gloucester regarded Salisbury in honour's equal reticency;
Watched, sought out a Restaurant and drank /civil/ brown tea,
Musing on elms long felled, /Constable/ George Borrow, and what
Might be taken all in one month gone over sea, /in/ /one month to
          be./

The Coin

It is hard to guess tales at once from sight of a thing,
Suddenly brought to the light, though one may have blood
Of Rome, all instinct, and quick to the makers mood.
So I could not tell, Constantine's coin, being upploughed;
What manner of man had lost it, with what regretting,
And not till music began in my mind it seemed
Possible to find out from a heart that dreamed
Day long of Rome, majesty and mildness in setting
Of Crickley curves against Severn, and clouds that streamed.
So, though it might have been the farmer that had lost,
Or mere private from the hillside missing beyond his cost
The casually let fall coin that not till now had gleamed
Above the shear of the plough, shown in the rubble of cutting.
Him I might have saluted, or round his shoulders
Put my arm – now could not be imagined, the horses surges
Went up and down the field, great bodies at strength held.
And the coin given me lay in my pocket, urges
Continual to take out the thing, and watch its so bold
Countenance of an Emperor, dust with all his friends that were,
But this symbol suddenly gathered from the many coloured mould.

The Coin

It is hard to guess tales from the sight of a thing
Brought up suddenly to the light though one may have blood
Of Rome, and as I, all instinct, quick to one's /high/ mood.
So Constantine's coin suddenly upward /turned here/ ploughed,
Still left me dumb of word as to what the loser seemed –
(Only in music my spirit rightly /mused or/ dreamed.)
And the Roman that lost this small penny-thing was most
A wonder to me, though Plutarch I had read, Virgil, and others;
/(English)/ I could not get to a comradeship of him, nor /make/ ring
The coin on stone as once he might have – but stared and stood
/Far off/ Watching the valley, the Welsh Hills, with a sting
Of regret (that I, war poet had lost /this high/ good
Of knowing one of my infinite dead generations of brothers –)
My arms might have lain friendly on ~~their~~ /his walking/ shoulders;
/His/ Spirit spoken to spirit of my deepest pondering ....
So following the plough under the lovely and ancient wood,
A coin was ploughed up, heating thought till it /sudden grew ruddy,/
      ~~hurt~~ and glowed.

A Strange thing

Coming out of three weeks trenches they cheered
(The Gloucesters) as winter rabbitts, hungry and starved,
Desiring tea, smoking, sitting warm by a fire.
They cheered – I laughed; one for one short moment was freer.
What was it? A girl, we had seen no woman at all for
Six weeks; strafed like blazes – and Hell cold like a bore.
Continually at one, for 12 hours, sentry-duty frore.
Watching over to Chaulnes in evil dark unstarred
In this worst time of trenches, far worse than we had feared .....
Had not expected such natural kindliness,
A girl coming to greet a Battallion - heart-friendliness.
For France coming to speak this gracious one daughter.
So the Land that writes poetry and fought Wattignies,
Sent us a herald - it was as if Cotswold, suddenly,
Had greeted us with dear love, giving all, no less.
As though Cotswold with our own girls, white ways beeches free
Had showed a grace of Roman to this other Roman
Land, now without grace – sodden with Winter water.
So Gloucester caught at goodness after the fashion of Gloucester.

The Strange thing

Coming /free/ out of 3 weeks trenches they cheered –
(The Gloucesters) weak and hungry as /winter/ rabbits, - starved
For tea, or wine or sitting warm smoking /easy/ by a fire –
They cheered, and I laughed, and got a short moment's fire.
What was it? A girl, we had seen ~~no~~ /never any/ woman for
Six weeks or so, and had been strafed and stood sentry frore
Watching over to Chaulnes in ~~the~~ /evil/ dark unstarred:
Stepping out from breakfast into three foot /frosted/ water;
(The worst time all of France – far worse than we had feared.)
And so this sight of France, this kind-heart daughter
Of the land that writes /clear/ poetry and fought fierce Wattignies –
We welcomed as though Cotswold suddenly /here/ had appeared;
/(smiling)/ With our own girls, above Artois flat plain here –
Would have broken ranks to kiss her, if we /dared/ had dared ....
So Gloucester caught at /lost/ humanity like old Gloucester.

Varennes

At Varennes also Gloucester men had their stay.
(Infantry again, of my soft job getting tired.)
Saw wonderful things of full day and of half-day:
Black pattern of twigs against the sunset dim fired.
Stars like quick inspiration of God in the seven oclock sky.
Where the Infantry drilled frozen-all all foolishly
As on the Plain – but to the Canteen went I,
Got there by high favour, having run, finished third,
In a mile race from Varennes to the next village end.
Canteen assisstant, with a special care for B Company –
And biscuits hidden for favour in a manner forbidden.
Lying about chocolate to C Company hammering the gate.
Pitying them for their Parade all the morning through
(Blue to the fingers, to all but the conscience blue)
Uselessly doing fatheaded things eternally.
But keeping (as was natural) Six Platoon ever in mind.
/((Until the anger of fire caught all, all in rose or gold was lost.))/

Varennes

~~At Varennes also Gloucester men had their stay;~~
~~(I had given up my soft job, like / — / Infantry reason — getting tired.)~~
~~And saw wonderful things of full day and half-day.~~
~~Twigs wonderful black /pattern/ against winter sunset fired;~~
~~And stars like the new thought of God /act/ in seven oclock sky.~~
~~Ploughland /as/ with the old trouble of man misted all melancholy.~~
~~And, lucky to escape, I got a post /(warmer than most)/~~
~~Of selling biscuits and other things in the warm/er/ aired~~
~~Canteen — while others "changed arms" in the blood stilling frost~~
~~Or did unhappy exercises /forlornly/ , smartly, unreasonably.~~
/Slept with them, praising fortune – in Duty and off Duty way./
And one evening, drowsed by the wood fire /(poet)/ I got lost in the
Blaze of warm embers, /green wood/ smoking ~~ever~~ annoyingly;
Watched deep till my soul in the magic was /rapt/ asleep;
Grew to power of music, and /all/ poetry, ~~and~~ /so/ uncared,
/(Loved)/ Became a maker among soldiers – /dear/ comrades;
Which is of the hardest of all /wide/ earth's many trades;
And /so/ proved my birth-right, in a minute of warm aired
Staring into the wood fire's poetic heart, lost a tide deep.

The Glad time

Moving south from Laventie, after May till October
In, we stayed at Robecq, ~~and~~ /over us/ passed Toussaints;
>Toussaints, sacred time, celebrated by peasants who
>Went dark clothed to mourn (through a glory of colour)
>The dead sons of the land fallen, save for France, in vain.
>It was the Day of Return, lit was plane and poplar;
~~All~~ /Earth/ light mist and azure, or glorious with the taper
Or ~~arrow~~ /arrow/ head leaves fallen stained from the /Roman-birth/
        ~~obeying~~ tree –
(Beauty, beauty was the there, /all-/grave, boy-heart, and sober.)
Lillers we reached and Doullens after a many /soldier/ chant
Of music hall or Gloucester /all/ or /of/ Army manner;
/Five months/ Having held a still line with ~~never~~ /no/ lack of honour;
Stood incredible pain of thirst, frost or /other/ want;
Now to go to the Somme to be mudhole soldiers /somehow,/ some-
        where –
But recovering ~~soldier~~ /Gloucester/ -pride from the freedom of
        marching, ~~and~~ the slant
Of countryside; the greeting of French people in honourable manner.
>And here to see Toussaints, the day of sorrow, gleaming
>Soft with the beauty of the year turning, setting us yearning
>For all the beech woods of Cotswold, leaves now downward streaming,
>This at Robecq miles past our usual border.
(O soldiers, how your pride rots, stuck still, /bearing,/ waiting order!)
We moved as soldiers of Rome moved when whim or want
Of soldiership moved an Army across Gaul - to our /unseen,
        unguessed/ ~~new~~ Front.

At Seaton Delaval

/At Depot, at/ Seaton Delaval the miners hearts were warm –
And the women, I believe, would have denied themselves for soldier's
        sakes.

Great blazes went up the /wide/ chimneys in homely flame,
And there were scones of different kinds, and fine home made cakes –
>James Pigg was remembered throwing scorn upon
>The Surrey farmer's mean fires, after the day's hurry and storm,
>Coming upon a lonely house, wet through, with his lean figure,
>And worn horse, needing rest after the day's unheeding
>Struggle through ~~hege~~ hedges, ditches for the found at last fox.
>So I remembered watching the great trouble of flame,
Any generosity given with North-Country charm.
Rough voices, but hospitality like any /of/ old-time farm.
There was our Depot, Hell in it's thoughts and ways,
Discipline harrying bare souls into revolt and hate's daze –
Hours like spinsters', bedtime when time was most of use.
But for three hours or so always free, /(save some duty)/
There was the goodness of the North miners /hospitable/ company –
Talking strange talk to ours, /theirs/ iron to soft South Country.
But the courtesy of the Severn valley and /spoilt/ Tyne plain,
So great in its goldenness 'twas much as the same.
>And a miner woman's kindness, lovely to have after the orders
>And reasonless bully-of-hours, never more courteous the lady
>Of some Castle of hospitality on ceremonial borders.
Lovely courtesy, with hot tea in the night's quiet free time.

Finding Red tiling

Ploughing red tiling up or finding it /loose/ scattered,
One wondered at the old villa life, at it's homeliness
And charm, before the spoilers tore apart there and shattered
The Roman house so beautiful ~~there~~ in it's /air-washed/ loneliness. –
Crickley with all West-Severn's tempests /equal hammered and / ~~so~~
            battered ....
>Where I for a while had a home, in the gleaming farm
>Of Spring, or glooming of Winter, in drifting hazes.
>Felled trees, tagged wood, led horses, did what was ordered;
>Wrapt in so much beauty – Briton, Roman nobleness

>Saw in my working (writing out often verses)
The fir copse, and the hallowed high clump of beeches.
Below the white farm in its beauty, and /strong/ time-worthiness.
With the meadows, great water ~~el~~ celandines /golden-strange/ in its
        reaches
Of Marshes – once the Roman boys and girls /happy/ made laughs
At conventions, and in the dear darkness had lover's /first/ kiss,
/(That first)/ The farmer loved his earth, her home the mistress;
Sentinels, soldiers knew the place talked, /exiled,/ far scattered;
Of the Crickley farm with its generosity and friendliness,
As of the first of all things /(exiled)/ to them that mattered.

"A talk in Company"

"Townshend, I /could/ wish William Byrd were /knighted,/ made a
        baronet.
For I have been to Westminster and heard /his/ music there ....
As noble as "Cataline" or any of our Shakespeare.
Better still for us, I wish he had been a free patron
And given /to/ Greene and Dekker and John Marston
Their true chance, and me more than a butt of /scanty/ red wine –
O[r] eighty pounds odd, title of Poet Laureate.
/Byrd –/ Great Latin greatly set to great music there ....
William Byrd, William Byrd, Companion of us, and master –
Would you watch with us at Phoenix talk/ing the/ all year's dawn?
>Sit with us talking poetry, hearing with your own mastery,
>And saying the true thing none other could have known.
>Guessing by instinct what the writer should have known pat,
>But by part ignorance , part knowledge in strange degree
>Mixed – /would have/ found the one thing we were questing at.
And talk sailor talk with men not come to /near sure/ disaster,
Because of the /brave/ god protects sailors and soldiers, making men.
But, /this/ Townshend, all this makes glory grow /stronger,/ ~~the~~ faster;
And stronger about this great age of stone and pen."
/What music squarely set to such iron grave Latin./

Epitaph on a Young Child

They will bury that fair body and cover you –
You shall be no more seen of the eyes of men,
Not again shall you search the woodlands, – not /ever/ again
For violets – the wind shall be no more dear lover of you.

Other children shall grow as fair, but not so dear,
And the cold spirited shall say "It is wrong that the body
Should be so beautiful" – O puritans /warped to/ moody!
You were the true darling of the earth of your shire.

And all the flowers you touched, but would /for pity not/ ~~not~~ pick,
In the next Spring shall regret you and on and /so/ on –
Whether you are born again your love shall not be done –
In the most wonderful April or October your spirit shall ~~yet~~ be mystic.

Dear body (it is an evil age) that /so/ enclosed
So lovely a spirit, generous, quick to anothers small pain;
Is it true you in the dark earth must be down-lain?
Are there no more smiles from you in the house, sunlight drowsed?

I must find out a Love to console my /hurt/ loneliness,
Forget your children's beauty in the conflict of days –
Until there come to me also the sweetness of some boy's
Or girl's beauty - a Western spirit in a loved coloured dress /of flesh/.

Chipping Campden

If they would only sing madrigals /now/ in the wide streets
Or the old songs of Cotswold these men's fathers sung –
It would perfect (and only perfect) the /so/ strong
Wonder of Elizabethan goodness that /still/ everywhere meets
The walker of Chipping Campden her houses /now, about,/ among.
Shapes perfect, great walls, and patterns like earth-sense strong;
Everywhere beauty and humanity stands /age-noble/ and greets
The wanderer to find Shakespeare's land or Shakespeare's tongue.

It was October, the creepers to infinite colours
Were turning, and of all beauty the /hurting/ unending dolours;
/(Melancholy)/ Frost the air sweetened, and the face there stung.
And for the orange windows, one had cried at the gates
(Or door/ways/ of dusk) "O let me in, let me in!
I also have read all the sweetness that "Winters Tale" sung –
And longed for company in the old places of Gloucester ways and
          sights.

Of George Chapman

After a screed of Iliad, from Southwark he walked out
Full of the glories of the Iliad, worked out of all doubt,
And saw Thames running in full water up to Kew ....
And ships floating or unloading with full-labouring crew;
Said "Thank God, some glory is added to my life's story.
London has given me honour after some coloured manner.
But Hertford, Hertford, if you would take me again,
(That bore me) and give me a farm stead, a life clear without
Any trouble of how to earn, or what to do .... /and/ now;
>With a wood of my own to cut, my own land to plough,
>Orchards so often azure for my own home cider –
>A spade, an axe, a pitch-fork, and a few horses.
>Enough money for them and my study's courses.
>Translating I would leave for another man, waiting
>Only when I should grieve, ~~at~~ for the English writing
>Of Greek however glorious. In my farmstead or manor.
Why, I would surpass Will Shakespeare in /drama/ ~~all play~~ of
          History,
And of Rome outdo /great/ Jonson for all his friend's clamour
Of "Cataline", "Sejanus" – and many a /(noble)/ number more he
Wrote (For all their greatness and state and arts' honour)
/Old Earth of/ Hertford call me home - I am sick of the tricks of the
          town.

The Unfamiliar Camp

Some day (I know) they will dig up the ramparts perhaps
To find money hidden or broken swords or spear tips –
And renew an old honour of tales, which now /(there a glow)/
Is but of comradeship with the stars and /unseen/ dew
Of dawn, the eternal watching to Welsh mountains and great tops.
But to me it will be /surely/ but the small camp left aside,
For the toil of the climbing, jumping of the brambles, and /so/ slow
Change of the love's colour there from May to May's return slow .....
(Wonderful colour staying long in drenched miraculous glow.)
>Many Romans have discovered there the first
>Violet, harebell has quivered its delicatest
>Shards, before some-elsewhere brave flowers durst.
>In exile thinking of the child-games and hurting tumbles
>Years ago, before Service came, one had had with one's sisters,
>Or friends, gathered all first things from early snow drops.
The one camp left aside of all my loved ones stretching wide ....
The friends who watch me at midnight must forgive me,
/Readily/ Because after climbing and brambles I hurry by;
See, there are the lights of Gloucester in the unbreathed ~~still~~ valley.

London Dandies

Having nothing better to do they will go to view
Shakespeare's new play – and it is "King Lear" and stiff History.
Anyway, bore or not, tobacco is cure for /all/ rue.
And what if the fool's mirth is to them strange mystery?
/Lear,/ Cordelia, Edgar, they all know (but not as we
Looking terribly with them to immortality.)
>The dandies catch a chance phrase of the Fool's and take
>Their tablets out; one smokes through his nose – while the gallery
>Save the rapt true ones, hear no more of accusations
>(All man's spirit) against immortal evil or folly,
>Than do idlest watchers by Thames for curiosity's sake –

>Though man turn god with trouble, conqueror through disaster.
>Though men weep seeing souls bound to rack all the faster,
>Nobleness shatter, evil achieve, and plain goodness shake.
But the sisters and Gloucester,
Kent, alone, proclaim Shakespeare Maker and master.
He is sitting near, it is not easy to know what to do
When a poet one admires is comrade of landlord of squires ....
God! but the fates bring all worthiness to disaster!
So one, who has Gloucester blood in his veins, he turns /him/ to
Warwick, and says "Sir, you shame us all with our /own/ shires.
Your verse so full of our bloods love and adoration true,
Our earth cries, give him homage above the lands old knights and peers.
/Our children's blood unborn cries out to you./

At Crucifix Corner

They passed us the Sussex men, and with strained faces –
Having marched far, to the historied and dreadful places
(Mudholes merely) of outposts and of first line.
(It was December time, there had been much rain.
Afterwards the Scots followed with easy march; hallowed
To me by long readings of Scott's and Burns' pages.
(It was great to be in an Army with Sussex and Argyll men).
>(Had they spoken words out of Scott or Kipling .....
>The words of their shires earth said, marching by us, wearied
>With long uselessness – silent, bearing arms instead.)
But still the cold and long nights and /Hell of/ mud's pain
(Where such I longed for a soft job,) and for the wages
/(evil)/ Of Dysentry and one time in I got it – and after
A freezing weeks fatigue on Somme's high chalk land –
Where, after a day or two ~~I had~~ /they gave soft/ official duties ......
To fill water carts, and ~~see~~ /inspect/ white stuff put in;
Got warmth of nights, and a dugout – /even/ in comfort wallowed
Compared with those my Gloucesters /(generous)/ who after hailed
Me as they passed to some other Hell of war hold, /in mud cold./

Where they might freeze or be rained on in night's damnable cold ...
Damnable misery, slippery ditches, poor wretches marching with
      light paces.
>After a week of it dysentry got me, I had dreadful miseries
>Of body-pains, chills racked me, I was sent to the mercies
>Of a forward Dressing station, and there got curlities
>Of blankets, warmth of sort after winter's unsheltered rages.
But I had a "job" - a soft job and wrote verses, verses
Of homelonging, and /some/ music too above the glimmering
Meres of Ancre; and of Gloucestershire made my verse praises;
/Watched,/ Tended water carts, Trespassed to Albert; and the cold
Defeated, when they could not, with such coke as raises
Almost as much coughing as the pain it displaces.
And talked with Scots engineers at their machine,
And with Argyll, Elgin, and men Hebridean –
Aberdeen, Inverness and the County of Perth;
While Gloucesters froze the mid-marrow /even/ of their bones;
Got no more pity than so many stocks or stones –
Watching winter stars majestic in their /high/ courses.
Or dun skies terrible to the high soldier courage even –
While to me /waiting/ the Fifty First brought Scottish phrases
Of delight with a clarinet and pipers, suddenly making fine
New Year's midnight with a joy long absent and /gold/ sign
Of a joy-in-making perhaps before long should be /made/ mine.

Palm

About the shores at Eastertide
The priests go out and gather wide
The palms of willow to deck shrines,
Will celebrate Spring and old Israel's scenes.

Instead of the spread palm, Orient-kind,
Severn gives white palm as soft as lined
Ever the cradles of princes of the high
Families of England, Chief earls of majesty.

Children, you shall watch with a new pride
The altar, spread in mannner all Gloucester-sacred:
"Will they not bring violets in March, and the great
Daffodills to give ~~the~~ old Ceremony ~~a new~~ golden state?"

"Will they not gather willowherb when the heat
Of the summer makes ~~all~~ Severn like a low-~~worn~~ street?
Priests, let us gather ~~purple~~ wealth of Michaelmas daisies
At the true time - to give God and Gloucestershire praises?

Only at Easter and Christmas they bring
Palm and holly - at Christmas still sing
Songs of the earth them in love brought ~~them~~ /to/ birth ....
Else is the year held in all worship from mirth.

. . . .

Christ was Born at Bethlehem,
St Francis in Italian ....
Pity and bless our Gloucestershire,
And grant our flowers their hearts desire.
/Let children rule and righten men./

Oxford

Long ago it was I first saw Her with /young/ eyes
Ignorant, and willing for any /rapture of/ worship –
But yet the true beauty of Her made me more wise
To honour of learning, and in honour of comradeship.
(The white stone and green waters with quietening trees.)
Since then I have read Buckley, and ~~greater~~ /in many places ~~finer~~/
          Belloc,
(And in the Line Shelley) and had the shock /given /
Of noble Greek ~~given~~ /writ/ out in noble /clear /English.
Read books of Oxford, ~~clear~~ /strict/ printed, ~~noble~~ /masterly/ of
          space;
~~A~~ /That/ "Dedicatory Ode" /and/ "Rewards and Fairies" –

And out of Edward Thomas got many a /dear/ wish,
But Her own beauty, quiet (in a quiet lack even
Of hills and heights;) yet stays with me, and the needed praise
Of our so honoured master /of all/ Robert Bridges.
(Lyrics and elegies worthy salutations of Jonson 's days.)
Oxford, you draw many hearts, and mine is one truest of these .....
Who had loved to acknowledge your name, your /fame, your dear-
            remembered/ Mastership.

Christopher Marlowe

With all that power he died, having done (his) nothing ....
And none of us are safe against such terrible proving
That time puts on men – Such power shown; so little done ....
Then the earth shut him out from the light of the sun.
All his tears, all his prayers to God, and Elizabethan loving
Gone to a nothing, before he was well of age –
Having seen Cornwall, perhaps visited /a loved/ Germany,
>(Gloucester will send heart out to like Canterbury,
>In the maker's heart was some likeness of clear striving)
Known all London, read /in/ many a poets page –
Brave and generous, braggart and generous /in/ doing,
Poet born and soldier, sobering to his elder age;
The earth covered him /~~from us~~/ and wrought wood was his
            clothing.
"Tamburlaine" half glorious, /then/ "Faustus", half victorious,
He left us, chief, an ache that a poet ~~of~~ /true/ man of men,
Should be stabbed cold, like any mean half gallant frothing;
            /nothing,/
Other men honoured, great ones made a tradition true,
>But we curse luck for silence in manners various –
>The courage and youth and virtue of Christopher Marlowe.
~~But we are poor, and curse luck how it may run /askew/.~~

In first May

In first May it ~~was~~ /seemed/ as natural ~~to~~ /for/ wandering by
Severn as to say Shakespeare to the trees and the sky:
As natural to choose "Midsummer Night's Dream" for that one –
As to walk, touch the brambles, [deletion] bathe in the sun,
                                        For love of the sun.

After Wainlodes, Haw Bridge, with past thought of hawthorn
And on past Foscombe Hill, where a tiny stream is born;
Hartpury with its tall elms, children coming /home/ from school.
In first May-time this was but the wanderer's ~~true~~ /natural/ right rule.

Gift after gift, and at Maisemore /height/ see the valley spread
With the noble Abbey, and the City, Cotswold Wall what was desired…

>The City of Zeus all glorious, or of Britain all melancholy,
>Or the Roman City set for war and peace guarding the valley –
>Thus under the range of Cotswold, seen after climbing from
            Hartpury.

This, all, was the gift, the common gift of Western Spring; /in its
            glorying,/
And to all men such joy casual chance each year /like first flowers/
            should bring.

Leaving a soft job

/Detached men,/ Hearing our Infantry were about to move,
Not satisfied with our comfort or our safety (in proof)
The desire also stirred us to ~~see~~ /company/ our Battallions,
Greet comrades again, and freeze with them in the ~~fire~~ /cut/ rough
Ditches of Picardy, Artois or of La Flandre …..
True, we were warm of nights, and heard not the violence
Of shells threatening imminent death on our dug-out's roof;
Hunger, and love-longing and /of/ soldiership /so/ commander,
We would bear no more our quiet, but made applications

To return to our regiments loved, whatever might be the chance.
Warwicks, Berks, Worcesters, or old /honoured/ Gloucesters.
Because honour is honour, this comfort /is/ not enough;
Not enough for the shame of safety without blame.
What though the lovely Ancre made marsh of /lucent/ wonder
At sunset /gloom/, what though freedom were remembered once
Clearer here, than with burnishing of straps and buttons?
The fame of colours, the glory of old battles called "ours" there ...
And Crucifix Corner it seemed better (a little) to leave,
Though afterwards we for candles and /such/ warmth might grieve.
Hoping a march at least with war-loved companions.
And in (at least) goodness of hardship again to believe.

After work

Often at after-midnight I have gone
Out into London,
Unable to work on.
And seen Westminster, and great Thames flowing there, ...
Wandered till Lockhart's opened and loneliness were done.
Thinking of Borrow, Boswell, and /be-/lovéd Shakespeare.
/(So many)/ But ~~the~~ craftsmen whose place of rest it was,
And ~~usual~~ /of/ drink and /night's/ meal, resented the newcomer as
Stranger to them; though student, (and war-poet
Did they but know it.)
London pride forbade any /other/ using the place;
Save he were one of craft, or to craft /bound/ apprentice.
So after a while, out of my hope I was done
And only seldom /warily/ came to Whitefriars Lane:
Who should have had the freedom of all friendliness clear;
Honour, Elizabethan memory, and a soldier's good welcome .....
Alas, to enter White Friars Lane with any fear? /Even there/
Will not poor men honour a maker ~~any more~~ /in heart/ again?

Talking under the stars

It was natural once to expect a /free/ time
Of walking with one
Who loved as I did the graces of music or rhyme,
My arm round his shoulder thrown.

And in sweet October together watch /blue/ orchards, deep
Past one's imagining
For beauty, or to feel the /dusk/ land settle ~~at dusk~~ to /comfort of/
          sleep;
~~Later the high~~ stars marching.

But what evil men call Time; (evil, plotting black evil)
Has taken all this,
And pain past bearing hour ~~on~~ /after/ hour on me still
Weighs past thought that is.

Cotswold promised all, France promised ~~me~~ /rewarding/ all,
~~My~~ /Of/ complete earned desires –
(So I should return) and accomplishment, praise of England still
Pay of my past-price cares.

All this is taken – my friend and the longing for warm
Talking in inn evenings ....
Who by Chaulnes ~~promised myself of all dear life the~~ /reckoned to
          myself payment of great/ charm
~~Of~~ /In/ natural, uncosting things.

Rye

I rode and saw the sea for first time – first,
After so many years, it was near Battle.
Passing so much lovely red tiling, and deep colouring –
(Hating my bicycle, fearing /sudden/ punctures accurst.).
Hearing or guessing of windmills the lovely rattle.
Then to Rye, finding the kindest faces of any company

Of all England (I thought) of /scattered/ kind Counties many.
Drank /brown/ tea – rested my body, and let settle
Peace into my mind after so much hard riding.
Then, too poor and adventurous to sleep in Company,
Went out and sought a rest place; ~~there was a~~ /at last found a/ wind-
        mill
Noble above the flats and near beach of pebble.
There I lay cold covering myself with the mockery
Of a macintosh I had brought – smoked and watched the stars turning
In their high courses, shivered with dawn showing /clear,/ pale –
Then rose to walk the beach till men should first stir and bring
Comradeliness into a world so lonely – watched full-day settle ....
Then Returned to Rye and hot tea, and what kindness might bring.
>But , O Sea port of England Old, O Cinque Port, little
>You rewarded me – riding so far and so hard –
>To shiver a night through, under no true shelter –
>Find pebble for a harbour – river for open port –
>My days were like that then, full of unpaid, scorned battle.

Upon Solway

Upon Solway they talked of the new /wide-honoured/ fame,
Coming to one Ben Jonson, and his Solway blood.
Wondered what money from London /to/ playwriting came, ...
And took great pride in his renown of Flanders soldier.
While he, buffetting /at/ feather beds in most angriest mood,
Called only on Solway /(exile)/ when anger heated to flame –
/(In Drama to his true strength growing the bolder)/
And bent at midnight to his new play with a heart all grieved
With the stupidity, /light/ cruelty of London, Patron and theatre.
(Longing to be North there /again/, and to hear his grandfather's
        name
Spoken with love by tongues of men ~~he had~~ /still known/ dear
In imagination, /to/ ploughman, craftsman and /lonely/ farmer.
To talk the night through ~~with them~~ /free hearted/ till nothing could

Remain to say of anything was wise, ~~or~~ /common or/ good .....
All gossip spoken – all praise of poetry or /noble/ blame.)
But he had no money, and no recognisance /ever/ came,
(Or not much – /not/ even to the play Shakespeare himself gave
       aiding)
No honour, no money, no chance of seeing the racing flood
Surge past sand-spit, headland, till the tide were at full height.
/(O London!)/ So from his own folk even Ben Jonson must be
       stranger.
>Though, after much privation, acting any station,
>Correcting plays and such, he had come to some good –
>An entry at the "Mermaid" – with 'prentice clubs in honour ....
>Company at "the Phoenix" after a play-loving night;
>Lodging in Southwark – where men's fame might last longer.

A chance meeting

Seeing the elver fishers light /on bank/ so dim (yet gold
Under the high bank; with a strangers whim /wearied/, odd,
I also turned my steps there and joined them ....
Four boys fishing for elvers at the height of flood.
Quiet Gloucestershire /set-to/ in workmanlike mood.
So they told me of their catches, and I snatches
Of war talk, freezing cold by Aubers, or Chaulnes /broken,/ when
Just such a time of night made the thought hard-hurt, turn home;
>To Severn, Severn villages, hill villages, This Severn.
Quiet they were, the true good Gloucestershire /tranquil/ mood;
And were not much stranger, nor kept many /cunning/ watches,
On their own words, for a soldier /tried/ I once had been;
>Of Right of the company of all men – whether small or great the
       catches.
So having right of /all/ company wherever men gathered.
Under the willows with them an hour perhaps I stayed ....
Then moved to Wainlode's, watched out for the things unseen ....

The great Welsh Border, and high Malvern, /(with colour smothered)/
Then went homeward, to write, if my pen or mind could.
A night of Elver fishing, but a true thing of West Gloucester & Severn.

Arras June 1917

In the front Line men frizzled, but I was /for once/ luckier;
And got shade, and some moving, and clear water
~~Got~~ /Drawn/ from a tiny river that ran very near.
In the unbearable heat it was ~~bad~~ /heavy/ for any,
But here, stuck in reserve /Line/, this B Company
Had right to bless the gods for a chance of naturally
Moving up and down ~~the Reserve line~~ /free for strolling,/ – clear
Unhindered for fifty yards – while the Front Line in gun batter,
Thirst, and intolerable waiting; too drowsed for chatter
Even, stayed ~~drowsed~~ /stifled/ in not bearable heat-drift of summer.
Such was the Front, luckier /one week/ than we were wont,
>Who had Grandcourt, Chaulnes to come, and Vermand Front.
B Company praised some humourous god for their better fate here,
Praising a bad luck for a rather preferable matter –
To move in stifle about the Second Line, /allowed/ rather
Than to lie nearer Fritz in an all damnable smother
Of heat – without movement, /without care,/ thinking little of fear.
O Gloucesters, ~~to come~~ /exiled/ so far to be broiled in a damned
Ditch, and this the war men write of in ~~a~~ London's daily newspaper!
>Some verses I wrote, and read, even music, however
>The week dragged over us it's dull weight – Talk no helper.

Song of Autumn

Music is clear about such freshness and colour,
    But how shall I get it?
There is great joy in walking to the quarry scar,
    And glory – I have had it.

Beech woods have given me /truest/ secrets, and the sighing
Firs I know, have told me
Truth of the ~~truth~~ /hearts/ of children, the lovers of making.
Old camps have called me.

It is time I should go out to ways older than tales,
Walk hard, and return
To write an evening and a night through with so many wills
Aiding me – ~~so~~ little now to learn.

~~Newnham on Severn~~

Newnham on Severn stands as high ever above
The world it seems, as any place of old high story.
Watching the wide flow of Severn with stilly love.
And Cotswold guarding the wide East with quarry and swarding.
>Romans came there, William loved it, and surely one Henry?
Watching, reflecting on old tale and imagining lost History,
(~~But~~ Newnham also ~~has had of arms it's~~ /of Civil War had/ danger
          and proof.)
She dreams low and mounts /high/ aloft to discover
Infinite beauties unthought of far hills or near river.
(And the day changes so, with ~~its~~ cloudy never resting roof, ...
And lovely unmatched varieties of shimmering colour
None of that earth can speak out his adoration or love.)
Like a girl's face all changes, and though ~~on the~~ /on red-earth/
          heights
One finds on ~~ruddy~~ /Farmland/ soil the earliest of violets ....
It is not so much .... the never ending ungrasped mystery
Of colour which hurts, and moves to tears with /finding and/ sweet
          hurting.

A Continuation

"Marlowe is slain" he said, "and this ~~his~~ /poem, Marlowe's,/
Poem must surely by some hand come to finish."
So took ~~his~~ pen ~~and~~ remembered the /heights and the/ ploughlands
Of all old Hertford in days when his country /boy/ hands
Were more given to /field/ delighting than to any writing.
(But knowledge of Homer had come since – /and/ ~~a~~ great poetic
             manner.)
"Marlowe is slain, but I can no more make false
Lovely images of boys-love than make the calls
Of cuckoo or blackbird, at Easter to be /near/ cheating
>From their trees or coppices birds to my snares, or by walls
>Set the nets (not daring cruelty) to make them prisoner.
I must take my own course, trust to chance, and my spirit's
Own way of making – /This/ "Hero and Leander" demands
A younger pen than mine it's ending to be inditing"
>A quicker heart than mine to beauty it's hurting. –
But sat and wrote ~~after~~ /Epilogue to/ that youthful manage
Of pen, his own square sort of thinking, his /man's-/way of
             making …
And remembering Hertford /~~county~~/ past, more than Marlowe past,
/(~~The~~ In blood)/ Made line on line till "Hero and Leander"
~~Was~~ /Grew/ finished – for a task without impatience or /unman-
             nered/ haste.
A boy's beginning, a man's ending, strange mix of poetry's wonder.

Maisemore

Whatever season, Maisemore ~~was~~ /country/ always /is/ kind:
Always showed flowers in multitudes of many sorts.
~~And~~ Surely had compact /of kisses/ with the South Western wind?
Beside the weir, with its music or great /water/ roar
/(Endless)/ ~~Or~~ by the haystack, or the /weather/ gleaming white
             Court's

Orchards, the earliest and dearest violets /careful/ one might find –
And in Autumn colours, past poets, the truthfullest enrapt words.
>Sang there the friendliest gathering of different sort birds –
>All year round, the score of flowers, though Winter frosts
>Hurt their roots, or the thawing with cruellest edged wind.
Kindest of Severn villages – Such pride, /truth of earth,/ ~~high~~
        /clear/-mind;
I had to think my father bore there, and he had youth there .....
It was the place of all music, with Severn and with
Great Cotswold guarding the East/ward/ sky always alive,
For bird and cottage and first or unexpected flower
Of Christmas - Maisemore was generous ~~beyond compare~~ /(~~a girl~~
        ~~might have such~~ / /as with a young girl's/ care.)
The village grave, the old Roads for ever wandering a-wind,
Might be remembered always from farthest ~~islands or ports~~
        /trenches, even in night clouded blind/.

Of a great builder

One wonders if he built ~~the~~ /his mind's/ one great Thing.
To be allowed freedom to have his /~~(after toil)~~ after/ fling
Of choice with smaller churches about the City ways.
(White stone once now dirtied, the smoke does /hang and/ so cling)
Sedate, noble, /casual,/ many have returned with praise
To far lands of these Churches in their near-hiding
Of being over-towered by newer merchant places, to obscure
The clean and right lines of ~~the fitting~~ /Defoe and Boswell their/
        churches,
Which, for the worship of good men was large enough, sure
And worthy enough; to remind of Boswell/'s page/ in ~~form and~~
        ~~colouring~~ colouring
//Form/ (~~Now~~ in our /own/ printing Farquhar, Sir John Fielding.)/
Monument and scarlet stain on the walls – /that calls/
/At once reverencing, honour of death, life. Surely those days/
>Of Edwards, Goldsmith, Beauclerc were more truthful and

>More worthy – Was there not Langton for a poet?
>"Irene" has the great phrase and does know it ....
>"The Lives" "The Dictionary" "Human Wishes" stand
>Imperfect but not of vanity to humanity.
>Men, poor walked streets all night and saw Paul's stand
>Grand against dawn – Men wept, not ashamed to see
/The anger, woe of others. /
~~Were plain and good of thought~~. Wren nobly planned and wrought –
The names of all his churches in a long string
Are but the sounding of a great builders praise – Here he has
A right of honour of a thousand years, and then outlasting.

The Fatigue

Barrages like all Hell's thunders were flung on us,
Guns, great or small, blood thirsty, they swung on us
Muzzles, and threw shells like dried peas on the one trench
In which Gloucesters were - burdens most heavy, /unhandy,/ slung
       on us.
>Biscuits and bully, water, all unhandy – needing carrying every inch.
(It was before the Somme, we were Northward –) And yet there came
More terrible onslaughts of steel and /high/ fire from the east,
Where Aubers was, where the first gracious sun had shone /down/
      on us;
Terrible, terrible battering, like a huge beast /fury increased./
Bloody minded to get his cruel will, his bitter /deep/ fang in us
And the fatigue ended, we turned keeping courage /all staunch,/
To find Fritz greedy still, not ended the /evil cannon's/ game –
Going downwards, fear (battled with) white-faced, /continuous,/
      strong on us,
>Doing silly things – carrying biscuits; hurting honour and frame.
Until we rounded a curve, and the guns must /now/ swerve;
We were too low /down,/ and too difficult this farther range.
Yet more fatigue, and fighting through fear, ~~and~~ /useless/ shame.
So we brought biscuits into the Laventie July Line /of no fame/.

Maps

With the "Poetes du Terroir," /reading,/ one's blood warms;
~~Reading such~~ /Lists of old/ noble names, and in Ireland, Scotland.
Names of all-poetry or like /soldier/ iron ring suddenly out.
One reaches for the map and sees Norway's /ridged/ strand;
Blackened with great title worthy /sailor/ sea and shore, ...
>Only in Pallas, one gets maps, biographies, verses,
>Lists of books, indications of Romances, poetries,
>With towns of birth of poets, some where with arms
>The Gloucesters went – and ~~found trees places~~ of many charms.
>But I know not the poetry, doubting even Loved France to be
>Maker of songs – even after ages of changes of wars and farms ....
>Yet here the maps, birthplaces, blackened and honoured clear.
>Shall one watch Italy so – and its length of varied honour know
Or Russia, great with mystery, unfamiliar History,
~~And~~ /(Dark to me)/ Hardly dares (Life denies so) read any more.
Only, my own villages have lovely quiet charms of ages
In names; as Windrush, Staunton and of Moreton Standish –
I am brave enough to turn pages /of maps/, towns where my own
        blood
~~Have~~ /Has/ gone, /west-out to/ Gloucester, Boston, ~~and~~ /or/ Long
        Island.
Hartford, Salem, Plymouth, ~~and~~ /or to/ strange Providence ....
Found after such wide sailing, water and wind in shout.
There men, after tyranny ~~had~~ /finding at last/ own mastery, ...
Coming to ~~land~~ /foreign/ earth given of names out-landish;
They stood; and summoning courage ~~and~~ building /as of England/
        their farms /steads/.
/(Remembering)/ Ploughed untouched earth, the Indian land
        ploughed.
I watch their maps as my eyes watch ~~my own~~ /books, or my own/
        hand /my heart leads/.

Stroud

Life might wrap around one there, I remember
Comrades marching with me speaking with all of Love,
Of Stroud, besides waterways, with white factories;
And smoky or great sunsets dying to /great/ ember,
In Autumn time when azure touched all things edges;
>"Dost remember kid, Dursley, in that December
>We beat Stonehouse at football – they had the lead
>At half time." "Dost remember what equal wages
>They paid at Frome Brewery 'fore it went to bankruptcy –
>And left a free night time for girls or running races –
>The night in Rodborough with the dark girls dost remember.
>Winning the cricket match from Stroud District villages.
Even the new streets with old romance were /made/ beautiful.
By Rouge Croix Stroud men spoke the kind ~~way~~ /fashion that/ girls
Had by Stroud, by Martinsart (cursing time's /bitter/ proof)
Talked of the nights of love, and of boy or girl victories;
Knowing the misery of this time, and Grandcourt /past Campaign/
                sombre,
To lie before us after passing through Death's Valley.
By the mill-places there rushes grow and /leaning/ sedges;
Birds sing long after Spring to prove Gloucester's masteries
Of kindness, and orchards ~~these are~~ /light-azure/, fruitful, without
                number.
Stroud-water in short fury /from the hills/ foams and swirls;
Stars make the queerest patterns near their /dim/ marges.
And Stroud on market days has friendliest of /Country/ Companies,
Out /of/ Stroud noblest of beeches grow on slopes and /stone/
                ledges ...

The Brooch

The farmer showed to me once a metal /strange/ thing,
Said " This was chieftain's brooch once and held his cloak,

Roman /(they say)/, I ploughed it up yonder in the field" .....
And how the centuries in my blood shouted and woke!
It is good to live in an old land where at /the time of/ ploughing ...
One may turn up a having of a man long dead.
Under the great rise there, by the /one/ beech clump ruled.
Long land, old earth, you hold ~~your~~ /close our/ blood as strong
As music, there is no sacrifice we would not make –
>Nor any midnight wandering whereof [deletion] we have dread,
To keep you Briton, Roman or /of/ Elizabethan.
Our hearts to you by all sacredness are /gathered and/ held
~~And~~ verse, music only from you we freely take, /or make,/
But how you hurt us, memories, thoughts that hot in us throng .....
So at a chieftain's brooch /(one sight)/, my memories were moving
To flood full – or else the old remembered /half-truths; the/ deep
              heart ache.
>At a chieftain's brooch, a coin ploughed up, or a piece of tiling
>Scattered about the ploughfield of the thousand year-old
>Farm – and the spring bird cries from the copse of ~~prou~~ /loving/,
>Where the marsh is, and the great celandines grow /in too-/
              violent gold.

Authors

The rich man Shakespeare, good playwright, /loved one,/ who shall
              follow?
All men's fancy he pleases, what will /this/ London allow?
Poor men we are, and must leave it." /And did leave/ till the fire
Of making /hidden under/ rose in them, drove them crazy;
With hunger of beauty, masterless /blood,/ great desire.
So Ford, Tourneur many another wrote, /desperate-thought./
(At dawn times seeing the chinks grow slowly white – plain so
It might not be denied, light /now/ was on Thames side.
At dawntime having attained honour by great /~~muscle~~ daunting ~~most~~
              honest/ labour.)
So actors many and playwrights without envy

Strove for a City's praise with true craft, ~~and hard thought~~ /most
        hardly wrought./
>Cursing the dandies, cursing the people would copy there
>Half baked screeds of drama, hurrying pencil till it made
>Wretched skreeks on slate – or any fools that might write
>Taking the authors wit, as a thing for their lazy trade
>Of lounging day through, till a sight or theatre
>Gave something to minds hardly ever else growing clear
>So friends of Heywood honest as carpenters wrote –
(Yet /one/ with an eye on money, another on the Gallery)
Who'd rather have heard the hounds and the huntsman's /far/ hollow
In quiet places of England, their birth/place,/ and sought
Happiness, than write for London, merchant and clown to delight.
For the hardness of servility, and to badness /of praise/ so easy.

The tale

"Our garrison was Cirencester, but occasionly order
Was given to relieve outposts of Chosen or nearer Crickley.
And once Painswick – a great camp first pride of spade and pick.
Where we might look out East to great Wales Her /line of/ border.
Once we /moved/ down to Gloucester where I saw /(their own law)/
Great piles of daffodills and willow palm /pale there/ brought by Britons,
To be sanctified with ceremony of all /high/ awe;
And to praise the coming of Spring in Her Western /and more/ quick
Way – and one British girl forgave conquest /for one time,/ ~~and~~
        kissed me;
For joy of the Springs coming, and that ~~there~~ /at home there/ had
        missed me
The dear tokens of the first year in North/ern/ Italy.
A kiss of Europe, a lovely kiss of comradeship I
Dared not return, – the child of the river ways and woodlands;
So spring came, and ~~we~~ my returning to Cotswold (more-exile) the
        harder.
/More hard the commands./

Ypres

North French air may make any flat land /dear and/ beautiful
But East of Ypres scarred was most foul and dreadful
With stuck tanks, ~~and~~ /ruined/ bodies needing quick /honour's/
          burial,
But yet sunset, first morning, hallowed all, /awed, made/ mysterious
The ugly curves of land running to eastward/; the Front/ of us,
Worse things of conflict not yet hidden ~~right~~ /unseen/ underground.
>(Shall we also fall stricken by one steel shard, sicken
>The air with stenches, ~~that were of the Gloucestershire villages,~~
>Be buried with haste, horror; by those were comrades before,
>Lie, covered, rot, with no hope but to make meadows quicken
>When Time has cleaned this dreadful earth of infinite brute
          carnages;
>And left some clean stuff; earth, beautiful – as once bodies were?)
But the place was most hideous at times, /of mankind all/ unheedful;
And we forgot all battle honour – all glory storial,
Our County's birth, (our great pride) that would make stir us,
Even on the brink of the grave to the risk of warfare.
Only the half lights wonder gave us remind /(made heart kind)/
Of the villages and dear households we had left /foolish and/ all-
          dutiful –
(But too rashly for such vile pain, and gray hideousness)
/At/ Ypres – the talk of soldiers was the one delight there.
~~And the~~ /The one goodness/ greatness of bearing Hell-from-high
          without fear.

Faces

Loving many faces I did not kiss,
Watching many manners I could not ~~but~~ /make/ miss,
Wasting spirit, honour, ~~and~~ /making/ strength in London,
Till torture and the uselessness made ~~me undone~~ /the will almost
          undone./

/There/ I yet saw, /in/ Northend Road, the happiest crowd,
And Paul's mountainous first about surging /urge of/ Fleet;
Thames with all colours and varying /other/ surges;
And though I had none, was happy ~~in~~ /seeing/ others fun –
Musing of making my own things walking (apart from this)
By Chelsea, where another, my Master, had gone for his proud
Strength to gather, his eloquence to cry hotly aloud.
>Who wore the diverse and the poetic true cloaks
>Carlyle, he; master of late night workers and
>Turner (lost to himself), Whistler painter of Thames in ebb or flood,
>And the painter of faces all might understand
>Carlyle, Turner, Whistler, the most cunning and true of hand.
>There, too poor for company of my right quality, I
Sat in a Saturday gallery, and saw the human
Enormous joy at clowns, clamour at ~~old~~ /too-often/ jokes;
Heard ragtime should bring the place /for riot/ with a sudden run
          down.
(Horribly racked perpetually with damned electricity –)
A maker – with but the midnight stars on the dim marges
Of Thames to comfort me, noble Hufflers with red sails taut –
Helpless with all a boy maker's surges and ~~urges~~ all of ambition's urges.

The Nightingales

Three I heard once together in Barrow Hill Copse –
At midnight, with a slip of moon, in a sort of dusk.
They were not shy, heard us, and continued uttering their notes.

But after "Adelaide" and the poets /ages of/ praise
How could I think such beautiful; or ~~gather the lies~~ /utter false the
          lies/
Fit for verse, it was only bird-song, a midnight strange new noise.

But a month before a laughing linnet /in the gold/ had sung
/(And green)/ As if poet or musician had never/ before/ true tongue
To tell out nature's magic with any truth ~~held~~ /kept for/ long .....

By Fretherne lane the linnet /(in the green)/ I shall not forget
/(Nor gold)/ The start of wonder – the joy to be so in debt
To beauty – to the hidden bird there in ~~elms /green/ great~~ /Spring
        elms elate./

Should I then lie, because at midnight one had nightingales,
Singing a mile off in the young oaks – that wake to look to Wales,
~~And~~ /Dream and/ watch Severn – like me, will tell no false /
        adoration in/ tales?

Doullens

At Doullens (only two days old /then)/ I saw a newspaper.
"The Observer" and lots of French papers hung up together ....
But dared not break ranks – a misdemeanour and dire caper
For infantry; so I stayed, and hurt; /sullen,/ marched /on/ eight more
Kilometres before they let us sink down on /golden/ straw ....
/Anger,/ And think of the lovely Bibliotheque Nationale
Small yellow volumes, six sous each, of Balzac and all
~~And many~~ /Hugo, Dumas,/ others of the great names of order and law
Of French making, in wonderful and cheapest /(late found) yellow/
        store.
No, they marched us by /all/, strict habit, and bright accoutre,
Through Doullens Town, books newspapers and friendly people –
Landing us at a small village of no ~~weight~~ /account/ whatever.
Where only the peasants, /drink,/ and ~~the~~ Rest, were kind; ~~and~~ one
        /had/ rather
~~Would~~ /Miss the books,/ miss the /damned/ daily paper than take
        the bother.
>Who had in my pack or trench tool holder but Keats,
>"Spirit of Man" – Walt Whitman – perhaps damnèd AEschylus.
>Some Shakespeare – some Wordsworth in penny editions, and
        Cobbetts
>"Rural Rides" – and "Wild Wales" – hidden somewhere in the
        general mess.
>(But O for Belloc, Bridges, and were it possible some Yeats.)

Chaulnes

They retreated, we passed there, /through/ most dreadful tangles of
        wire ....
(Impregnable it seemed ~~to~~ /with/ any of Infantry fire.)
~~And~~ passed the damned Pillboxes, ~~and~~ /concrete places,/ wonder
        how Fritz
Could give up such a position; and all in bits
Everything was; knocked flat by such devil-of /evil/ war ......
As for near three years had hurt Artois, /Picardy,/ with mortal hurt.
Later, we found our comrades grave, they had buried him ......
(Found his body, loved his face, carefully had carried him/, tended
        him/.)
And heard the words of commemoration said ceremonious over
The white cross and the little mound; Europe /even now/ had care
Of Europe; this great spirit killed in the /reckless/ night;
~~Was~~ Buried with /danger's/ tenderness by his loving enemies.
The Gloucesters watching the cross, craftsman's work, past their loss
Remembered gratitude, and praised chivalry for this
/True-/Burial of a comrade loved best of all the companies.
Honoured the care had fashioned so honourable a cross.
>And forgot our grief, but not hunger in noble billets
>Of Omiecourt, where much wood was, and there I found many
        postcards
>Of German towns nailed up for memory's rewards,
>Two great books of plainsong in noble print with the wets
>And dirts of perhaps two Winters blotting notes and words.
>Hunger and fatigue, clear county after the wires and the bullets.

No Mans Land

Too afraid myself I watched that Gloucester ~~boy~~ /Lance Corporal/ go
Hunting a bird; in the first full light he had fired
At and killed; Partridges /in a flock/ or some such things.
Who returned in triumph, and dinner completed conquest so dared.

Strange to kill one's own meat, strange to see one /so/ little feared
To go out to the wires; ... this opposite warning of grim Aubers...
Where there were families and /competent/ flats of snipers.
Too daring .... but he was of Gloucester's /driven/ best and would
Have dared all that a Cotswold man ever thought he should –
Whether in open battle, or ~~the~~ damnable /trench-waiting;/ strict
        wired.
(But O how strange to see partridges done in by those
~~Who dared not think of such~~ /Bound careful to use of bread,/
        though from ~~the~~ /that/ County whose
~~Would~~ Woods were thick with such – and rabbits /white-tailed/ ran
        the ways.)
>He was but a lance corporal, to[o] nice for stripes,
>Whose jokes lasted longer in the rain or the frost,
>Than any almost – was to fall like so many of those
>At Ypres – where I watched them going up to the gaps
>Of wire – a machine gunner on sentry – in the smoke they were
        lost.

Dawns I have seen

Terribly for mystery or glory dawns have arisen
Over Cotswold in great light, or beginning /of/ colour,
And my body at them has trembled, for beauty /enraptured/ shaken.
(My spirit for so long Beauty's /friend,/ truest follower.)
It seemed the right of Severn to call from the East-heaving
Of Cotswold, nobleness his own for his right of honour;
And the birds have exulted as if newly let from prison.
To those dawns have I read Shakespeare, and the grand wide reason
Of Milton – the childlike wonder of Chaucer almost /on/ grieving
At the beauty of /dewy/ daisies in the /~~first~~/ May-time season.
Dawn over powering me past my own power of making;
Glorious as ~~the~~ West Country ~~is in~~ /dawns show,/ days first most-
        sacred hour.
No music in me to fit that great life-in-flood awakening,

To walk only, ~~on~~ /in/ other men's poetry ~~depending, there~~
Saying my heart in passion /out/ ~~and~~ /or deep/ musing.

Cotswold and Valley

Rome cries out from the hills – "This is all mine ever!"
And the valley says "Briton, who ever /else of blood/ has come here."
There are the ways of Danes – Saxons seem ~~not~~ /never/ to matter –
Who from their great fjords sailed south, /welcoming Spring,/ ~~and~~
            would discover
A warmer land, a kinder Land than that gray Northern Mother.
>Yet remembering their Great Sagas and dark stormy tales
>Of adventure of courage – or brother set against brother
>For the love of a woman, Winter had made dear in her wiles
But Rome having built Her camps, standing out against Heaven's
            lamps;
Haunt of the /one/ kite, the rabbit, the lonely plover,
Still holds the heart more than any that came /stranger ~~(though~~
            ~~conquering)~~/after.
(It is my own Country - it is ~~most~~ /West Country,/ noble Gloucester)
And when in France with such /birth/ I was comrade-soldier –
~~With~~ men handy with plough or with white wood, /hay or wheat,/
            clever,
>Knowing my blood Briton, Roman, my name Norman,
>A maker, remembering always a maker no bolder
>Should be than caution – till growing tired or growing colder
>I took careless the risks of the first – hurt beyond caring.
I saw time on time these things show their /old/ truth there.
Roman, Briton or Dane in the eye or ~~the~~ /dark/ hair or manner –
Whether in march strain, or rest, or ~~the~~ battle /strain or/ fever –
It showed ... the one nobility of my County Gloucester,
            Of that West, Gloucester.

The Lost Things

Who tore those plays, what careless actors; /(hurried)/ what cooks?
What street-stall sellers the /desired/ plays we have not in our books?
John Marston, great one, where are your /looked-for/ ~~high~~ /high/
       things gone?
There is "Eastward Ho" /now/ to prove with what manly looks
London of Elizabeth's time fronted the day that shone
Golden with colour and adventure before the /day's/ hours were
      ~~done~~ /begun –/
~~That brought them studious to the candle and the ink holder;~~
>("What! not to outdo "Catiline" – not write "Hamlet" more fine?
>Is Webster alone to surprise with beauty the soul of the eyes?
>All honour to master, must we always serve George Chapman?
>Or follow with love the nobility of John Marston?")
No time to all glory of verse /or/ sound ever ~~more~~ /worked/ bolder.
(And all those poets used to men's affronts and knocks)
There are twenty plays we dare not miss – /For mastery;/ no, not one
Of twenty; yet nothing remains of them in books, /rumour,/ or talks.
Great histories – Heaven accusing tragedies, /of gardens,/ lovely
      comedies .....
Gone out into forgetfulness like the flocks, /dark of looks,/
Of Starlings that whirr in Autumn suddenly from hidden rucks;
And come no more ever to the valley ~~the high white tower oversees~~
      the high white tower guards and oversees.

The Last of the book

There is nothing for me, Poetry, who was the child of joy,
But to work out ~~the~~ /in verse/ crazes of my untold pain;
In verse which shall recall the rightness of ~~my~~ /a former day./

And /of/ Beauty, that has command of many gods; in vain
Have I written, imploring your help, ~~you~~ /who/ have let destroy
A servant of yours, by evil men birth better at once had slain.

And for my County, God knows my heart, /Land,/ men to me
Were dear there, I was friend also of very /look of/ sun or rain;
It has betrayed as evil women ~~betray~~ /wantonly/ a man their toy.

Soldiers' praise I had earned having suffered soldier's pain,
And the great honour of song in the battle's first /gray/ show –
Honour was bound to me ~~she it~~ /save mine/ most dreadfully stain.

Rapt heart, once, hills I wandered /alone/, joy was comrade ~~then~~
          /there, though/
Little of what I needed, was in my power: again – again
Hours I recall, dazed with pain like a /still/ weight ~~downed~~ /set to
          my woe./

Blood, birth, long remembrance, my County, /all these/ have saven
Little of my being from dreadfullest hurt, the old gods have no
Pity – or long ago I should /have/ got good, they would have battled
          my high right plain.

Introduction to Notes

The notes to the poems have the following structure: the page reference and title are followed by an indication of the publication history of the poem. We have used the symbol ● to note when the poem is here published for the first time. If the poem has already been published, we list significant previous publications (we have not thought it useful to pursue the poems through anthologies or quotation in critical articles, or to list part-quotation of the poems as in Michael Hurd's *The Ordeal of Ivor Gurney*). Most published texts of poems from these collections derive from the notebooks themselves or from typescript copies taken from them, and we have noted where this is not the case. Publication information is followed by a list of all other manuscript and typescript versions of the poem in a conjectural chronological order, so that the researcher can easily make comparisons. The notes to each poem are those which are specific to that poem. We have also made annotated groups of names and places, and two maps, one of Gloucester and the surrounding area and one of the area of the Western Front, as the most succinct way of giving information on the people and the places to which Gurney repeatedly refers, and on the subjects to which he consistently returns.

We have used the date of publication to refer to the places where poems have been previously published, as follows:

1954 *Poems by Ivor Gurney*, principally selected from unpublished manuscripts with a memoir by Edmund Blunden (Hutchinson).

1973 *Poems of Ivor Gurney 1890–1937*, with an Introduction by Edmund Blunden and a Bibliographical note by Leonard Clark (Chatto & Windus).

1980 *The Faber Book of Poems and Places*, edited with an Introduction by Geoffrey Grigson (Faber and Faber).

1982 *Collected Poems of Ivor Gurney*, chosen, edited and with an Introduction by P.J. Kavanagh (Oxford University Press).

1985 Liz Ward, 'An Introduction to Ivor Gurney', *Words* vol.1, No.1 (June).

1986 Charles Tomlinson, 'Ivor Gurney's "Best poems"', *Times Literary Supplement*, 3 January.

1989 Liz Ward, 'Clear Lamps and Dim Stars: "New" Poems by Ivor Gurney', *Stand* vol.33, No.2 (Summer).

1990 *Ivor Gurney: Selected Poems*, selected and Introduced by P.J. Kavanagh (Oxford University Press). This includes some revisions.

Manuscript and typescript variants.

We have used a two-part citation for the manuscripts and typescripts to give two different sorts of information. The first element of the citation represents the group of papers from which the individual document originally comes and the second represents the present location in the Gurney Archive in Gloucester. It is essential to use this two-part system because the actual documents have been used for a variety of purposes and ordered and re-ordered according to different principles, and the original relationship of some groups has been obscured by their wide dispersal in the archive. George Walter's painstaking researches on paper and typing have substantially established their original groupings. We have used abbreviations based either on who might have been involved in the texts' production or on some distinctive feature of the paper used. Carbon copies are indicated by an asterisk.

Manuscripts and typescripts of *Best poems.*

Best poems is obviously an attempt to bring together a representative selection of poems, but it is impossible to define the exact relationship between earlier versions and the completed collection. This is partly because of the inexactness of dating of Gurney's manuscripts but more because of his habit of rewriting a poem rather than revising. He may for example write a whole new poem based on the inspiration, the title, the first line, or the first stanza of an earlier text. The following groups of manuscripts relate in some way to the *Best poems* text:

LS An undated manuscript written in blue ink on two small sheets of unlined paper.

1EB }
2EB } Undated manuscripts written in black ink on pages torn from exercise books.

3EB An undated manuscript written in black ink on a page torn from an exercise book. Perhaps part of 4EB.

4EB Undated manuscripts in black ink on a collection of pages torn from an exercise book and joined together.

1MAR A blue 'Marspen' brand school exercise book containing manuscripts in black ink. Two dated poems ('Winter Night 1925' and 'Victory Day 1925') date this in or after November 1925.

2MAR A blue 'Marspen' brand school exercise book containing manuscripts in black ink. Undated but containing drafts of poems in 1MAR.

A number of typescripts were made from *Best poems* after its completion, including one set that was seen and corrected by Gurney himself. The existence of copies made by John Haines and the lack of copies in Marion Scott's 1928 selection prepared for Gollancz suggest that the exercise book we are using was in Haines's keeping for some time before it was passed on to Ralph Vaughan Williams, who had it copied in 1943. The typescripts are as follows:

IBG A set of typescripts on flimsy foolscap paper, extensively corrected by Gurney in black ink. One of the notes and appeals which are written on these copies asks '(Mr) Gordon Canning' to petition the Carnegie Trustees for the publication of Gurney's 1924 award-winning piece *The Western Playland*. The earliest review of this on 1 May 1926 gives us a latest date for these corrections.

1VL A group of typescripts on paper with a vertical line wiremark, reproducing the texts of various typescript poems corrected by Gurney. Undated.

2VL A group of typescripts on paper with a vertical line wiremark, reproducing eight of the first nine texts of the book, suggesting an aborted transcription of the whole notebook. Undated.

HL Two sheets of paper with a horizontal line wiremark,

containing the first twenty eight and a half lines of one poem. Undated.

RVW   Originally an entire transcription of *Best poems* produced by 'a very good typist in Dorking' in 1943 at Ralph Vaughan Williams' instigation. The title page reads 'POEMS | –by– | IVOR GURNEY' and bears the note in pencil by Edmund Blunden: 'I have taken out for selection these, | p.6 The Lightning Storm | 7 I saw French once | 22 O Tan-Faced Prairie Boy | 31 The Silent One | 67 Song | 74 War Books'. The whereabouts of the texts Blunden extracted are unknown.

LC   A set of typescripts and printed material assembled by Leonard Clark in the early 1970s for his edition of Gurney's poems.

Manuscripts and typescripts of *The book of Five makings*.
There are no manuscripts which feed into the texts of *The book of Five makings* in the Gurney Archive, but there are manuscript transcriptions by Marion Scott and various typescripts produced after February 1925, though there is no evidence that Gurney had a part in the creation of these. They are indicated as follows:

EXC   A set of typescripts on 'Excelsior Fine' watermark paper with a title page in Marion Scott's hand, which reads: 'Poems which are ~~among~~ /selected/ from a set written by Ivor Gurney | in 1925 | in the bright pink marbled book | entitled by Gurney | "The book of Five Makings"'. Undated but conjecturally April 1926.

VL   Typescripts of the first three poems of the collection on paper with a vertical line wiremark. Undated.

MMS   A group of manuscripts in Marion Scott's hand on large loose sheets of plain paper. The first page is headed 'Gurney's Poems' and the group reproduces poems from a variety of sources, suggesting it was produced for the proposed Gollancz edition of Gurney's work that Marion Scott was working on in 1928 (see Chronology).

LUD   Four separate sequences of typewritten poems on 'Ludgate' watermark paper taken from the MMS transcripts. Presumably Mollie Hart's typing (see Chronology).

GF   Eight typescripts on 'Excelsior' watermark paper. Undated, but similar to the typescript copies of poems from the *London Mercury* that Gerald Finzi made in June 1937.

Notes to *Best poems*

To the memory of Alan Seeger (p.29.) • *Other versions*: 4EB 53.45v-46a, 2VL 42.2.48-50, 2VL 42.2.51-53*, HL 52.11.108, HL 52.11.107*, RVW 21.29a-29b*. *Notes*: Alan Seeger (1888-1916) published *Poems* in the year of his death on the Somme. See *Letters*, pp.278-9 for Gurney's reading of Seeger's best-known poem, 'I have a rendezvous with Death' in July 1917. 'Mannahattan' is Whitman's version of the name.

The Reward – and the earnings (p.30.) • *Other versions*: 1MAR 64.8.4v-5, 2MAR 64.7.3-3v, 2VL 42.2.72-73, RVW 21.30*. *Notes*: The last two lines are numbered 5 and 6 and written up the side of the page.

To the City of Rome (p.31.) • *Other versions*: 2VL 42.2.91, 2VL 42.2.92*, RVW 21.31*.

The Sudden Storm (p.32.) • *Other versions*: 2VL 42.2.96, 2VL 42.2.97*, RVW 21.32*. 4EB 53.46q, 'The Storm at Night', is an earlier poem which uses similar ideas; see *CP*, p.171. *Notes*: See *Letters* p.319 for his mistaking the Aurora Borealis for a coast bombardment.

The Lightning Storm (p.32.) 1954, 1982. *No other versions*.

I saw French once (p.33.) 1954, 1973, 1982 (not in *London Mercury*, as has been stated). *Other versions*: 2VL 42.2.37-39, 2VL 42.2.40-42*. *Notes*: See *Ordeal* p.61 for an account of French's review of the Gloucesters. There were numerous biographies of Sir John French (1852-1925) available; we cannot say which Gurney used, but his information is accurate. Marshal Joseph Joffre (1852-1931) was Commander-in-Chief of the French armies.

A London memory (p.35.) • *Other versions*: 2VL 42.2.16-18, 2VL 42.2.19-21*, RVW 21.33*. *Notes*: Many of the names, in spite of Gurney's mistake with Enobarbus, are from *Antony and Cleopatra*.

The County's Bastion (p.36.) 1982. *Other versions*: 4EB 53.46c, 2VL 42.2.89, 2VL 42.2.90*, RVW 21.34*.

After thoughts of fear (p.37.) • *Other versions*: 2VL 42.2.69, RVW 21.35*. *Notes*: The song he mentions making is 'By a Bierside'.

Honour (p.38.) ● *Other versions*: RVW 21.36*.

Ford spoke a word (p.38.) ● *Other versions*: RVW 21.37*. *Notes*: Shakespeare's sonnets speak truth as do the psalms of David (whose name Gurney connects with his father).

Hazlitt (p.39.) ● *Other versions*: RVW 21.38*, LC 65.35, LC 60.22*.

Ben Jonson (p.40.) ● *Other versions*: RVW 21.39*, LC 65.141, LC 60.54*. *Notes*: Gurney alludes to Jonson's *Bartholomew Fair*.

Song (p.41.) 1982, 1990 (from the 2MAR text). *Other versions*: 1MAR 64.8.8-8v, 2MAR 64.7.4-4v, RVW 21.40*. 'Minnewerfers' are trench mortars.

Of Peasants (p.41.) ● *Other versions*: RVW 21.41*, LC 65.127, LC 60.48*.

Of Grandcourt (p.42.) 1982, 1990. *Other versions*: RVW 21.42*, LC 65.40, LC 60.24*.

May the companion (p.43.) ● *Other versions*: RVW 21.43*.

On the First Army (p.43.) ● *Other versions*: RVW 21.44*. *Notes*: 'No mans' is No man's land.

O Tan-faced Prairie Boy (p.44.) 1954, 1982. *No other versions*. *Notes*: The title is from Whitman's poem in *Drum-Taps* (1865).

After Sunset (p.45.) ● *Other versions*: 4EB 53.46k-46l, RVW 21.45*, LC 65.39, LC 60.23*. *Notes*: Gurney was always interested in folk song, and this poem expresses how it marks various memories for him: the singing of 'David of the White Rock' by the Welsh (see 'First Time In' in *CP* p.69); the singing of 'The Farmer's Boy' on marches during the days of training at Chelmsford and Danbury. 'Seventeen Come Sunday' and 'Tarry Trowsers' are Somerset songs. On the 'soft job' with the water-carts in December 1916/ January 1917 Gurney met two Scots engineers who sang 'O why left I my hame', 'Ae Waukin O', 'John Anderson' and 'McGregor's Gathering'. See *Letters* pp.177 and 183.

The First Violets (p.45.) ● *Other versions*: RVW 21.46*, LC 65.140. *Notes*: The reference is to Margaret Hunt, whose house in Wellington Street helped foster Gurney's work, and whose room had the Bechstein piano and the Holbein reproduction. See *Ordeal* p.17.

Drum taps (p.46.) ● *Other versions*: RVW 21.47*. *Notes*: The title is another homage to Whitman, but a literal response, remembering the places where Gurney's company moved in 1915-17. Gurney mentions the bugle sounding 'Retreat' in his poem 'Hail and Farewell', which he sent to Marion Scott on 3 February 1917 and published in *Severn & Somme*. See *Letters* p.199.

City of Ships (p.46.) ● *Other versions*: RVW 21.48*. *Notes*: Another title from Whitman's *Drum-Taps*.

~~*Dirge for*~~ */Picture of/ two Veterans* (p.47.) 1989. *Other versions*: RVW 21.49* *Notes*: Whitman's *Drum-Taps* includes 'Dirge for Two Veterans'.

Dirge for two striplings (p.47.) • *Other versions*: RVW 21.50*, LC 65.42, LC 60.25*. *Notes*: Blythe in Northumberland was where one of the soldiers came from.

I saw Her soul (p.48.) • *Other versions*: RVW 21.51*. *Notes*: Bartholomew were the well-known map-makers. John Fountain appears in Lamb's *Specimens of English Dramatic Poetry* and Gurney's poem called 'John Fountain' (GA 17.108*) has the line: 'John Fountain's Extract – Lamb's book has nothing better'.

Sailor (p.49.) • *Other versions*: 4EB 53.46d, RVW 21.52*. *Notes*: Gurney was always enthusiastic about sailing, whether in the Dorothy, the boat he shared with Harvey, or in conversation with Nielson (see *Letters* pp.345-6), or intending to join ship after the war.

The Silent One (p.49.) 1954, 1973, 1982, 1990. *Other versions*: 2MAR 64.7.11.

Scabious and Trefoil (p.50.) • *Other versions*: 4EB 53.46r-46s, RVW 21.53*. *Notes*: It is not clear which boys' book about Classical heroes Gurney is referring to nor even which heroes.

The room of two candles (p.51.) • *Other versions*: RVW 21.54*.

Iliad and Badminton (p.52.) • *Other versions*: RVW 21.55*. *Notes*: Tothill Fields was a place for archery practice in Elizabethan times. Gurney is making a characteristic comparison of sporting (mainly cricket), intellectual, military and artistic skills. The cricketers are G.L. Jessop of Gloucestershire (1874-1955), Sir J.B. Hobbs (1882-1963) and H. Strudwick (1880-1970), who played together for Surrey, W.G. Grace (1848-1915), a Gloucestershire cricketer who would have been old when Gurney saw him, C.L. Townsend (1876-1958) who played for Gloucestershire, K.S. Ranjitsinhji, (1872-1933) who later became HH the Jam Sahib of Nawanagar, either R.C.N. Palairet (1871-1955) or L.C.H. Palairet (1870-1933), who both played for Somerset, Arthur Shrewsbury (1856-1903) of Nottinghamshire, and W.G. Grace junior (1874-1905) who played for Gloucestershire. Musicians like Fritz Kreisler (1875-1962), writers like Shirley, Boswell, Froissart, painters like Whistler, ancient heroes like Hector and Troilus are all part of the same sense of skill which the war has dimmed. Merton and Thornbury may be places where cricket was played.

Afterwards (p.53.) • *Other versions*: 4EB 53.46b, RVW 21.56*. *Notes*: The names of Smith, Robinson and Green are among the commonest English names, but soldiers in Gurney's company with these names died in March 1918. In the 4EB version, Gurney mentions Hancocks, Braine and Green who are much more obviously comrades who died: Corporal L.D. Hancocks (d. 23 August 1917), Lance Corporal H.P.G. Brain (d. 25 September 1916), and perhaps Private E. Green (d. 31 March 1918).

Lance Corporal (p.53.) ● *Other versions*: RVW 21.57*. *Notes*: This refers to Lance Corporal (later Corporal) L.D. Hancocks, who died at Ypres on 23 August 1917, to whom Gurney refers in other poems in these collections: 'No Mans Land' and 'To a Friend'. See also previous note and 'Farewell' in *CP* pp.170-171.

[Untitled] (p.54.) 1973, 1982. *Other versions*: RVW 21.58(1)-58(2)*, LC 65.138*.

Birds (p.56.) ● *Other versions*: RVW 21.59*, LC 65.67, LC 60.28*. *Notes*: Emily and Margaret Hunt lived in Wellington Street, Gloucester.

Greene (p.57.) ● *Other versions*: RVW 21.60*. *Notes*: Morley does not record any imprisonment of Greene, whom Gurney is using to express his own feelings of indignation at ungratefulness. Perhaps Gurney is confusing Greene with Dekker, who had constant money problems and was in the King's Bench Prison from 1613-19. George Chapman's translation of the Iliad impressed Gurney: 'By Gum, but Chapman's Homer's *Iliad* is immense! Better than all but the very great Beethoven.' *Letters* p.510.

The noble wars of Troy (p.58.) 1982. *Other versions*: 4EB 53.46p, IBG 52.11.93, RVW 21.61*.

Christmas night (p.58.) ● *Other versions*: 1EB 52.11.95, 3EB 64.12.369, IBG 52.11.112, RVW 21.62*.

Felling a tree (p.59.) 1982, 1990. *Other versions*: IBG 52.11.35, RVW 21.63(a)-63(b)*. *Notes*: Fabius Maximus (d.203 B.C.) saved Rome from conquest by Hannibal by strategic evasion of battle.

Prelude (p.61.) 1982 (from the 2MAR text). *Other versions*: 2MAR 64.7.5v-6v, RVW 21.64(a)-64(b)*.

Ballad for honour (p.63.) ● *Other versions*: RVW 21.65(a)-65(c)*.

Song (p.66.) ● *Other versions*: RVW 21.66*.

London Bridge (p.66.) ● *Other versions*: RVW 21.67*.

London Bridge (p.67.) ● *Other versions*: RVW 21.68*. *Notes*: Gurney worked in a cold storage depot in August 1921.

Of Death (p.67.) ● *Other versions*: RVW 21.69(a)-69(b)*. *Notes*: Gurney's 'By a Bierside' was composed at the Front in August 1916 and is certainly a song 'of ending'. His poem 'The Strong Thing' was written in December 1916 in the vicinity of Aveluy and speaks of death. Gurney's letter of 22 December 1916 to Marion Scott contains the text of 'The Strong Thing' and mentions the battalion standing 'in frozen mud to the knees'. He was wounded in the arm on 7 April 1917 and gassed at St Julien on 10 September. The early poem 'Bach and the Sentry' (see *CP* p.32) brings together October, Bach, stars and soldiering.

Humility – and Her friend (p.69.) ● *Other versions*: RVW 21.70*. *Notes*: Gurney associates various writers with places where he has read them. The setting of Whitman is probably Vaughan Williams's *Sea Symphony*, upon first hearing which Gurney was 'almost speechless from the shock of joy' (*Ordeal* p.35).

The Far Horns (p.70.) ● *Other versions*: RVW 21.71*.

Love (p.71.) ● *Other versions*: IBG 52.11.155, RVW 21.72*, LC 65.136, LC 60.53*. *Notes*: Another poem remembering the help given by Margaret Hunt. Eridanus is a constellation named after a mythological river (probably the Po). 'The Long Island book' is Whitman's *Leaves of Grass*.

At the time (p.72.) 1989. *Other versions*: RVW 21.73*.

A bit from my "Gloucestershire Rhapsody" (p.72.) ● *Other versions*: 4EB 53.46j, RVW 21.74*, LC 65.135, LC 60.52*. *Notes*: Gurney's 'Gloucestershire Rhapsody for Orchestra' is in the Gurney Archive at GA 25.9 and is dated 1919-1921. The 'Lament Song' is 'David of the White Rock'; see 'After Sunset' above.

Happy is he, Ulysses (p.73.) ● *Other versions*: RVW 21.75*. *Notes*: A more optimistic view of his own work. Gurney had contributed to a memorial tribute, 'Charles Villiers Stanford. By some of his Pupils', in *Music and Letters*, vol.V, 3, July 1924. The 'great gentleman' is Ben Jonson; see the poem of that name below. Gough Square and Bolt Court are associated with Samuel Johnson.

Southwark (p.73.) ● *Other versions*: RVW 21.76*. *Notes*: Gurney worked in a cold storage depot in August 1921; see the second 'London Bridge' above. Professor Henry Morley wrote of Drayton and Daniel but, though he mentions their forms, did not emphasise strictness.

The Elements (p.74.) 1973, 1982. *Other versions*: RVW 21.77*, LC 65.134*. *Notes*: The three overtures for Beethoven's *Fidelio* are known in English as Leonora and for Gurney have the magnificence of Gloucester Cathedral, St. Peter's.

All Souls Day (p.75.) ● *Other versions*: LS 52.11.138, 2EB 52.11.128, RVW 21.78*. *Notes*: All Souls Day is 2 November; 'Poilus' are the French 'Tommies'.

The Great Gentleman (p.76.) ● *Other versions*: RVW 21.79*. *Notes*: Gurney is again exploring his own problems of recognition and desire for reward in the person of one of the Elizabethans. Here it is Ben Jonson, who talks of his own tragedy *Catiline*, of Joachim Du Bellay and his patroness Marguerite de Savoie, of Beaumont and Fletcher's *Knight of the Burning Pestle*, and Thomas Dekker's *The Roaring Girl*.

Ely (p.77.) ● *Other versions*: 4EB 53.46i, RVW 21.80*. *Notes*: The writer of French blood is almost certainly Belloc.

Song (p.78.) 1954, 1973, 1982, 1990. *No other versions.*

To a friend (p.78.) ● *Other versions*: 4EB 53.46n, IBG 42.3.12, 1VL 21.87, 1VL 42.3.136*, RVW 21.81*. *Notes*: Compare 'The Battle', *CP* p.172, dated March 1925.

Elizabethans (p.80.) ● *Other versions*: RVW 21.83*. *Notes*: *The Alchemist* is the play by Jonson, whom Gurney mis-spells, *The Roaring Girl* is the comedy by Thomas Middleton and Thomas Dekker, and the other play is probably Thomas Heywood's *The Fair Maid of the West, or A Girl worth Gold.*

The Poets of my County (p.80.) 1973, 1982. *Other versions*: RVW 21.84*, LC 65.41*. *Notes*: Of the seven poets referred to, it is easy to identify the first as F.W. Harvey (1888-1957), and the second as John Masefield (1878-1967). The third may be Lascelles Abercrombie (1881-1938), whose *The Sale of Saint Thomas* Gurney took 'to be the best modern poem of ours' (*Letters* p.538) and the fourth obviously John Taylor the 'water-poet' (1580-1653). The last, who wrote of Rupert Brooke, is Wilfrid Wilson Gibson (1878-1962), whose book *Friends* was a great favourite of Gurney's. Leonard Clark put Abercrombie's name against the lines describing the fifth and sixth poets, and Abercrombie did write 'Ryton Firs', published in *Georgian Poetry 1920-1922*. W.H. Davies could be the third poet if Abercrombie becomes the sixth. W.E. Henley (1849-1903) seems a possibility for the fifth poet.

Portrait of a Coward (p.81.) 1989. *Other versions*: RVW 21.85*.

Cry of the People (p.82.) ● *Other versions*: RVW 21.86*.

Of the Sea (p.82.) 1986. *Other versions*: RVW 21.87*. *Notes*: Gurney visited Cornwall with Ethel Voynich in December 1918 and wrote on Boxing Day: 'And today we have seen great chasms, climbed rock of granite covered with lichen, and seen the sea quiet and gray, save near the rocks over which it boiled furiously when the mood took us. O a murderous but gloriously majestic place! The fear of men of the sea, but to poets a joy, a great memory after the seeing. This was Zennor Bay (I think) near Galver and West of St Ives' (*Letters* p.470). Gurney refers to his favourite authors on the sea, his own experience on the Severn, and quotes from Whitman's 'In Cabin'd Ships at Sea'. On 10 February 1925 he writes that 'There is besides, a setting of "In Cabined Ships at Sea" magnificent, for Piano, SQ Baritone . . . (one of W.W.s most high and difficult things)' (GA 46.2.2).

War books (p.83.) 1954,1982. *No other versions.*

Sounds (p.84.) ● *Other versions*: 4EB 53.46e-46h, RVW 21.88-90*. *Notes*: In response to Edward Thomas's 'Words'. Gurney wrote in August 1918 that 'Dear things like "The Trumpet" and "Choose me you English words" hang long in the mind' (*Letters* p.441). "Spanish Sailors" and "Tarry Trowsers" are folk songs; the Ninth, and Eroica are Beethoven Symphonies, while the *Sea Symphony* is by Vaughan Williams. The C minor is Symphony number 1 by Brahms (born in Hamburg, moved to Vienna), often thought of as Beethoven's tenth, and therefore neighbour to the ninth.

Notes to *The book of Five makings*

First poem (p.91.) . 1954, 1973, 1982, 1990. *Other versions*: EXC 12.1.1, EXC 12.2.6*, VL 42.2.65, MMS 64.11.130, LUD 12.4.42*, LUD 21A.156*, LUD 12.7.132, LUD 12.7.101*.

Thoughts (p.92.) • *Other versions*: VL 42.2.85, VL 42.2.86*. *Notes*: On 7 February 1925 Bumpus were paid six shillings for a Chaucer for Gurney (GA 11.1.2), and on 23 March Gurney set 'Merciles Beaute'. On 11 December 1924 Hachette were paid four shillings and fourpence for 'French books asked for by Gurney' (GA 11.1.2) and there are three settings of French songs dated 3 March 1925 one of which is labelled 'Chanson de Terroir' (GA 31.6.10, and see 'Maps'). There are several poems with the title 'Thoughts' in *Leaves of Grass*. *Voces Intimae* is Sibelius's string quartet.

Thoughts (p.93.) • *Other versions*: VL 42.2.87, VL 42.2.88*

October in Exile (p.94.) • *No other versions*. *Notes*: Toussaints is All Saints' Day, 1 November

October in Exile (p.95.) • *No other versions*.

Elizabethans (p.96.) • *No other versions*.

Elizabethans (p.97.) • *No other versions*.

From Laventie Line (p.98.) • *Other versions*: GF 21.21*.

So few places we went to (p.99.) • *No other versions*.

Like Hebridean (p.100.) 1954,1982. *Other versions*: EXC 12.1.7, EXC 12.2.5*, MMS 64.11.126, LUD 12.7.133, LUD 12.5.57*, LUD 12.7.95*, LUD 12.4.36*. *Notes*: Felix Mendelssohn's 'Hebrides' overture is the likely inspiration or parallel. For Zennor in Cornwall, see 'Of the Sea', p.82 above.

"Hebridean" (p.101.) • *No other versions*.

Salisbury Close (p.102.) • *No other versions*. *Notes*: See *Letters* p.82 for Gurney's visit with Cridland to Salisbury in May 1916. Salisbury was a frequent subject for John Constable's paintings and Edward Thomas's prose. When Herbert Howells was appointed assistant organist to Salisbury Cathedral, Gurney wrote on 11 March 1917 'How well I remember that exquisite Close with the Cathedral so delicate and yet so strong soaring like a pure desire.' *Letters* p.225.

Salisbury Close (p.103.) • *No other versions*.

The Coin (p.104.) 1973, 1982. *Other versions*: GF 21.10*. *Notes*: Gurney reports finding a coin in a letter of 22 April 1919 (*Letters* p.481).

The Coin (p.105.) 1982 (Notes), 1990. *Other versions*: GF 21.10a*.

A Strange thing (p.106.) • *No other versions*. *Notes*: Wattignies, south of Lille, was the scene of Jourdan's victory over the Austrians on 16 October 1793.

The Strange thing (p.107.) • *No other versions*.

Varennes (p.108.) 1982, 1990 (both texts insert the undeleted lines from the following poem between lines 16 and 17). *No other versions*.

Varennes (p.109.) See above. An arrow from above the line "Watched deep till my soul . . ." indicates that this part of the poem is to be connected to the revised version before the final line (written in pencil). See *CP* p.188 and note.

The Glad time (p.110.) • *No other versions*. *Notes*: Toussaints is All Saints' Day, 1 November.

At Seaton Delaval (p.110.) • *No other versions*. *Notes*: James Pigg was a huntsman hired by John Jorrocks in R.S. Surtees' *Handley Cross* (1843).

Finding Red tiling (p.111.) • *No other versions*.

"A talk in Company" (p.112.) • *No other versions*. *Notes*: Sir Robert Townshend was Jonson's patron. Manningham's diary for February 1602 records that 'Ben Jonson the poet now lives upon one Townshend, and scorns the world.'

Epitaph on a Young Child (p.113.) 1954, 1973, 1982. *Other versions*: EXC 12.1.3-4, EXC 12.2.3-4*, EXC 21A.170-171*, MMS 64.11.130v, LUD 12.4.40*, LUD 12.5.61*, LUD 12.7.120, LUD 12.7.99*.

Chipping Campden (p.113.) • *No other versions*. *Notes*: Chipping Campden is notable for its early buildings and is on the White Way from Cirencester to Stratford upon Avon.

Of George Chapman (p.114.) • *No other versions*.

The Unfamiliar Camp (p.115.) • *No other versions*.

London Dandies (p.115.) • *Other versions*: GF 21.4*.

At Crucifix Corner (p.116.) • *No other versions*. *Notes*: this poem is dated 'Feb 20th'. Compare 'Crucifix Corner' in *CP* pp.80–81.

Palm (p.117.) 1985. *Other versions*: EXC 12.1.5-6, EXC 21.1*, MMS 64.11.127-127v, LUD 21.1, LUD 12.4.38*, LUD 12.7.131, LUD 12.5.59*, LUD 12.7.97*.

Oxford (p.118.) • *No other versions*. *Notes*: see letter of 11 November 1919 (*Letters* p.499) reporting his visit to John Masefield at Oxford with F.W. Harvey. He notes that Bridges, Graves and Nichols were neighbours on Boar's Hill. The 'Dedicatory Ode' may possibly be Dryden's 'Prologue to the University of Oxford'. Kipling's *Rewards and Fairies* (1910) was the sequel to *Puck of Pook's Hill*.

Christopher Marlowe (p.119.) 1954,1973,1982. *Other versions*: EXC 21A.173, EXC 21A.172*, EXC 12.4.34*, MMS 64.11.127, LUD 12.4.39*, LUD 12.5.60*, LUD 12.7.121, LUD 12.7.98*.

In first May (p.120.) • *No other versions.*

Leaving a soft job (p.120.) • *No other versions. Notes:* The last line is taken from the foot of the facing page and there is no authorial indication of its placing.

After work (p.121.) • *No other versions.*

Talking under the stars (p.122.) • *No other versions.*

Rye (p.122.) • *No other versions.*

Upon Solway (p.123.) • *No other versions.*

A chance meeting (p.124.) • *No other versions.*

Arras June 1917 (p.125.) • *No other versions.*

Song of Autumn (p.125.) 1982, 1990. • *Other versions*: EXC 12.1.2. MMS 64.11.130, LUD 21.15, LUD 12.4.41*, LUD 12.7.125, LUD 12.5.62*, LUD 12.7.100*.

Newnham on Severn (p.126.) • *No other versions. Notes:* William I ordered Domesday Book in Gloucester in 1084.

A Continuation (p.127.) • *No other versions. Notes* According to Henry Petowe, Marlowe was writing 'Hero and Leander' at the time of his death. George Chapman's continuation was published in 1598.

Maisemore (p.127.) • *No other versions. Notes:* Gurney's father grew up in Maisemore.

Of a great builder (p.128.) • *No other versions. Notes:* It will clarify Gurney's amendments to explain that he first wrote:

> And worthy enough; to remind of Boswell in form and colouring
> Monument and scarlet stain on the walls – Surely those days
> Were plain and good of thought.

Gurney is obviously basing much of this on Boswell's *Life of Johnson*. Sir John Fielding (d.1780) was the Bow Street magistrate brother of Henry, the novelist. Thomas Edwards (1699-1757) was the Shakespearean critic. Oliver Goldsmith (1730-74), the Hon. Topham Beauclerc (1739-80) and Bennet Langton (1696-1769) were all friends of Dr. Johnson.

The Fatigue (p.129.) • *No other versions.*

Maps (p.130.) • *No other versions. Notes:* For 'Poetes du Terroir' see note to 'Thoughts' above.

Stroud (p.131.) • *No other versions.*

The Brooch (p.131.) • *No other versions.*

Authors (p.132.) • *No other versions.*

The tale (p.133.) • *No other versions. Notes:* Cirencester occupies the site of

Corinium, an important military station of the Romans.

Ypres (p.134.) ● *Other versions*: GF 65.66, GF 21.16*.

Faces (p.134.) ● *No other versions. Notes*: Hufflers are Thames barges.

The Nightingales (p.135.) 1982. *Other versions*: EXC 12.1.8, EXC 12.7.1*, MMS 64.11.126v, LUD 12.7.128, LUD 12.7.96*, LUD 21.24, LUD 12.4.37*, LUD 12.5.58*. *Notes*: 'Adelaide' is a song by Beethoven to words by Friedrich von Matthisson.

Doullens (p.136.) ● *No other versions. Notes*: The last five lines above are from the facing page. There is no indication of their place in the text, but they seem like a continuation in spite of the full stop.

Chaulnes (p.137.) ● *Other versions*: GF 21.23*. *Notes*: The last six lines are from the facing page. There is no indication of their place in the text, but they seem like a continuation. The subject is Richard Rhodes; see *Letters* p.239.

No Mans Land (p.137.) ● *No other versions. Notes*: The last five lines are from the facing page. Again there is no indication of their place in the text, but they seem like a continuation. Compare 'To a Friend' and 'Lance Corporal' in *Best Poems*. Lance Corporal Leonard Dodd Hancocks died at Ypres on 23 August 1917 (see 'Farewell' in *CP* pp.170-171).

Dawns I have seen (p.138.) 1980, 1982. *Other versions*: GF 21.22*.

Cotswold and Valley (p.139.) ● *No other versions.*

The Lost Things (p.140.) ● *No other versions. Notes*: The last seven words are on the opposite page without indication of where they should go.

The Last of the book (p.140.) 1954, 1973, 1982, 1990. *No other versions.*

Names and Places

We had originally planned to include a glossary of the names and places in this book; but when we had completed it, it seemed unattractively repetitious. In particular, we seemed to be repeating: 'Gloucestershire village or hill, familiar to Gurney in his walks' or 'French town or village to which Gurney's battalion went in 1916-17'. We therefore decided to make a virtue of the repetition and to collect together the names and places into thematically-connected groups. This not only deals with the subject succinctly but also emphasises the central areas of Gurney's concern in the asylum period. Details which are not part of these larger areas, or which need more specific information are dealt with in the notes to the individual poems.

The list of topics of *Best poems*, where he describes the poems as 'of New England/ of City of Gloucester/ of Embankment/ of Aldgate/ City of Bristol/ Tewkesbury/ Others', is suggestive of his interest in America, Gloucestershire, London, but it is not definitive. Gurney's ideas do indeed cluster around particular topics, and he returns often to similar ground. There are seven major areas of interest in the two books of poems in this book:

1. The France of Gurney's war experience.
2. The Gloucester area to which he always felt he belonged (often called Cotswold).
3. The Elizabethans whom he read avidly, with whom he identified to some extent and on whom he projected his own problems.
4. London, which mixes his own experience as a student at the Royal College of Music with the locations associated with the dramatists of the Elizabethan and Jacobean theatre.
5. Gurney's reading and the arts in general.
6. America, particularly as represented by and in Walt Whitman, whose *Leaves of Grass* is called 'the Long Island book', and who influences Gurney's geography.
7. The stars, to which he often turned as emblems of permanence.

The areas interrelate, and one might add Roman history, perceived as lying beneath Gloucester's character in the same way as the past more and more fully inhabits the present for Gurney. But the seven should suffice.

Gurney's wartime France

The map of Gurney's France opposite shows the places to which Gurney was moved during his time at the Front, and the Chronology indicates his movements. Gurney sometimes refers to the region, as in Artois, Picardy, or Flanders. He often indicates the place by the name of the river, as in Ancre, Lys, Scarpe or Somme, but usually it is the name of the nearest town or village which he uses to locate his experience. It can sometimes be difficult to tie dates to places since his letters were censored deliberately to eliminate any reference to place, and A.F. Barnes's *The Story of the 2/5th Battalion Gloucestershire Regiment 1914-1918* can be helpful here. The towns and villages referred to are the following:

Albert
Ancre (river running near where
    Gurney had his 'soft job')
Arras
Artois
Aubers
Aveluy
Belloy-en-Santerre
Béthune
Boulogne
Chaulnes
Campaign
Corbie Ridge
Crucifix Corner (location in
    Neuve Chappelle)
Doullens
Dunkerque
Estaires
Fauquissart
Flanders or La Flandre
Gommecourt
Gonnehem

Grandcourt
La Gorgues (Gurney's usual
    spelling of La Gorgue; the site
    of brigade headquarters in
    Autumn 1916.)
Laventie
Lillers
Martinsart
Merville
Mons
Neuve Chappelle
Omiecourt
Ovillers
Richebourg
Robecq
Rouen
Rouge Croix
St Omer
Tilleloy
Varennes
Vermand
Ypres

Map of Gurney's France

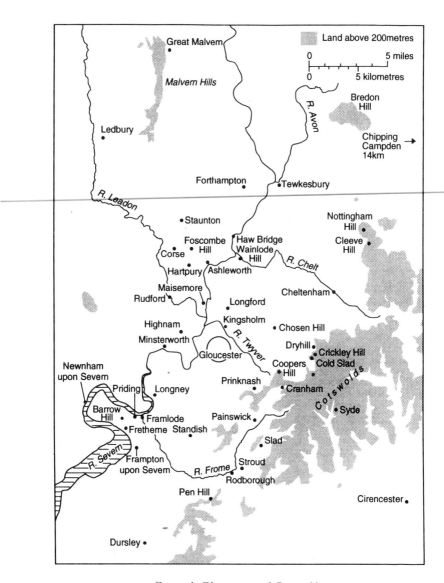

Gurney's Gloucester and Cotswolds

Gloucester and Cotswolds

Gurney's most frequent way of referring to his native county and the surrounding area is to call it the Cotswolds (he refers to the Cotswolds over fifty times in the course of these two books), but the hills, villages, towns and rivers of his youthful experience provide many of the landmarks of his mind. Again the map opposite is the most useful way of indicating Gurney's personal geography. There are some English names which refer not to the Cotswolds but to places which he visited either on musical business (like Durham), or as a soldier in training (like Chelmsford, Tidworth and Salisbury Plain). When he saw Ely is difficult to establish. It is interesting to see how many places Gurney mentions are hills; in 'Strange Service', Gurney writes to England of 'Your hills not only hills, but friends of mine and kindly' (*CP* p.31). The following places are shown on the map:

Avon	Foscombe Hill	Nottingham Hill
Barrow Hill Copse	Framilode	Painswick
Bredon (Hill)	Fretherne	Penn (Pen Hill)
Chosen (Hill)	Frome	Priding
Cirencester	Hartpury	Prinknash
Cleeve (Hill)	Haw Bridge	Rodborough
Coopers Hill	Kingsholm	Rudford
Corse	Leadon	Side (Syde)
Cotswold (Hills)	Longford	Slad
Cranham	Longney	Staunton
Crickley (Hill)	Maisemore	Stroud
Dryhill	Malvern Hills	Twyver
Dursley	(Moreton) Standish	Wainlode (Hill)
Forthampton	Newnham on Severn	

Elizabethans

Gurney was fascinated by the Elizabethan and Jacobean playwrights, and they form a frequent subject for his poems. They are not only a subject, but also a company in which he includes himself, and one often senses that Gurney is exploring his own problems of recognition, of craft and of identity through their voices. In April 1926 he even finished a pastiche Elizabethan play, *The Tewkesbury Trial* (GA 42.8). He associated himself with Ben Jonson by simple parallels: where Jonson had talked with Drummond of Hawthornden, Gurney had been in love with Annie Nelson Drummond and refers to her as 'Hawthornden'. Gurney remembers that Jonson also fought in Flanders. It is because of the association with them that he at times attributes to Elizabethans opinions and events which did not happen; the most obvious of these is the suggestion that Greene was in prison for debt for seven years (though this may be a mistake for Dekker). But Gurney did read avidly in the playwrights, particularly in the books edited by Professor Henry Morley. One cannot be certain which of Morley's numerous collections, histories or editions Gurney bought for half a crown in 'Elizabethans' (see p.80), but he could have read extracts from Greene, Beaumont and Fletcher, Ford, Chapman, Webster, Marlowe, Heywood and others in Morley's *English Plays* volume of Cassell's 'Library of English Literature'. Gurney often refers to authors by their places of birth, so these have been added below where relevant to the poems.

The Alchemist Ben Jonson's comedy (1610).

Bartholomew The patron saint of *Bartholomew Fair*, subject of Jonson's play (1614).

William Byrd (1538?-1623), musician, organist of the Chapel-Royal and publisher of, for example, *Liber primus* and *Liber secundus Sacrarum Cantionum* (1589 and 1591).

Cataline Jonson's play (1611; Gurney's usual spelling of *Catiline*).

George Chapman (1559?-1634?), born in Hertfordshire, chiefly known for his translation of Homer, but also a dramatist, and author of a continuation of Marlowe's 'Hero and Leander' (1598).

Thomas Dekker (1570?-1632), dramatist, author of *The Shoemaker's Holiday* and collaborator in *The Roaring Girl* (1611) among others.

Faustus *Doctor Faustus* (1588), Marlowe's tragedy.

John Ford (1586?-1640?), dramatist of whose life little is known, but who is most famous for his *'Tis Pity She's a Whore* (1631).

Robert Greene (1560?-1592), playwright and pamphleteer.

'Hero and Leander' Marlowe's poem, left incomplete at his death in

1593 and completed by Chapman (1598).

Hertford native county of Chapman.

Thomas Heywood (1574?-1641), dramatist best known for *A Woman Killed with Kindness* (1603) and *The Fair Maid of the West, or A Girl worth Gold* (pub. 1631).

Ben Jonson (1572-1637), dramatist of Border descent and so associated with the Solway and Galloway by Gurney; did military service in Flanders. Gurney refers to his comedies *The Alchemist* (1610), *Bartholomew Fair* (1614), and his tragedies *Sejanus* (1603) and *Catiline* (1611). Not only his quality but his stubborn belief in his superior talent may have endeared him to Gurney.

Christopher Marlowe (1564-1593), dramatist, born in Canterbury, author of *Tamburlaine* (1587) and *Doctor Faustus* (1601?).

John Marston (1575-1634), dramatist, author of *The Malcontent* (1604) and with Chapman and Jonson of *Eastward Ho!* (1605) for which they were briefly imprisoned.

Mermaid The tavern in Bread Street frequented by poets and dramatists.

Morley Professor Henry Morley (1838-1923) of University College London, prolific editor, literary historian and selector of English literature.

Phoenix A theatre adapted from a cockpit in St. Giles-in-the-Fields.

Sejanus See Jonson.

James Shirley (1596-1666), dramatist, author of comedies, tragedies and masques.

Solway River between Scotland and Cumberland, associated with Ben Jonson.

Tamburlaine See Marlowe.

Cyril Tourneur (1575?-1626), of whose life little is known; author of *The Revenger's Tragedy* (1607?) and perhaps *The Atheist's Tragedy* (1611).

London

Gurney's London is a mixture of the London of his own experiences as a student and places associated with Elizabethan dramatists and other literary figures.

Aldgate London street and the principal east gate of the city, also mentioned in, for example, 'The Road', published in *The Spectator* on 31 March 1923. Chaucer once occupied the gatehouse.

Fleet Appropriately for Gurney, both river and street, leading up Ludgate Hill to St. Paul's.

Knightsbridge Fashionable district between Hyde Park and Kensington.

Lockharts A London restaurant or tea-shop.

Mayfair The smart quarter of London at the turn of the century, north of Piccadilly.

Northend Road Road near Gurney's Earl's Court digs.

(Saint) Paul's Wren's cathedral, at the top of Ludgate Hill.

Southwark A London borough at the south end of London Bridge, famous as the site of ancient inns and theatres, the Globe, the Hope and the Rose.

Whitefriars Lane Street running from Fleet Street to the Embankment.

Gurney's reading

Gurney was an avid reader before he went into the asylum and he continued the habit there, supplied by Marion Scott. Much of his reading reinforces discoveries made much earlier, such as Whitman and Belloc, but his reading of the Elizabethans and the classics was developed. The following authors and books are mentioned in the poems.

Aeschylus (525-456B.C.), the Athenian tragic poet. Gurney admired in the trenches John Stuart Blackie's translation of *The Lyrical Dramas of Aeschylus* (1906). See *Letters* p.148-9.

Hilaire Belloc (1870-1953), essayist and travel writer, born in France. His *The Path to Rome* (1902) was a favourite book of Gurney's.

George Borrow (1803-1881), linguist, translator, traveller and author; Gurney wrote on 31 August 1917 that 'Today I have been reading *The Bible in Spain*, that brilliant curious book. Indeed, but Borrow is indispensable – *Lavengro*, *Wild Wales*, *Romany Rye* and *The Bible in Spain*! A queer chap though, and often purposely queer.' *Letters* p.318.

James Boswell (1740-1795), Samuel Johnson's biographer.

Robert Bridges (1844-1930), poet, and Poet Laureate from 1913. His anthology *The Spirit of Man* (1916), especially since Gurney had F.W. Harvey's copy when it appeared that Harvey might have been killed, was very important to Gurney.

Theodore Alois Buckley Editor of Pope's *Iliad* and *Odyssey* who published his own literal translations in 1851.

Thomas Carlyle (1795-1881), historian and essayist, author of *Heroes and Hero-Worship* (1841), *Past and Present* (1843) and *Sartor Resartus* (1833-4), whose style Gurney found used 'words alive'.

William Cobbett (1763-1835); Gurney was most impressed by *Rural Rides* (1830), both for its walking and for its quality of English. See *Letters* p.225.

W. H. Davies (1871-1940), poet and autobiographer. Most famous for his *Autobiography of a Super-Tramp* (1908), though Gurney admired his early poetry in *Nature Poems* (1908), *Farewell to Poesy* (1910), *Songs of Joy* (1911), and *Foliage* (1913).

Daniel Defoe (1660-1731), author of *Robinson Crusoe* (1719).

Alexandre Dumas (1803-1870), French dramatist and novelist.

George Farquhar (1678-1707), author of *The Beaux' Stratagem* (1707).

Henry Fielding (1707-1754), novelist, author of *Tom Jones* (1749) and *Joseph Andrews* (1742).

William Hazlitt (1778-1830), essayist, author of *Table Talk* (1821-2) and *The Spirit of the Age* (1825) etc. W.C. Hazlitt's *Memoirs of William Hazlitt* (1867) report his last words as 'Well, I've had a happy life'.

Victor Hugo (1802-1885), French poet and novelist

'Human Wishes' Samuel Johnson's poem 'The Vanity of Human Wishes' (1749).

Iliad The Greek epic poem, which gave Gurney a way of uniting literature and war, past and present. He read it in Chapman's version and also in Buckley's, it seems.

Irene See Johnson.

Francis Jammes (1868-1938), French poet and writer of short stories.

Samuel Johnson (1709-1784), lexicographer, poet, man of letters.

His play *Irene* was put on by Garrick in 1749, the year when Johnson published 'The Vanity of Human Wishes'.

Louis Petit de Julleville French critic; Gurney may well have used his *Morceaux choisis des auteurs francaises, poètes et prosateurs*, (Paris, 1912).

Rudyard Kipling (1865-1936), poet, short story writer and novelist. Gurney admired his *Puck of Pook's Hill* (1906) and *Rewards and Fairies* (1910).

Charles Lamb (1775-1834), essayist, and editor of *Specimens of English Dramatic Poets* (1808) which provided Gurney with much of his familiarity with earlier dramatists. The madness of both Charles and his sister Mary may have given Gurney a particular sense of kinship.

Captain Frederick Marryatt (1792-1848), wrote energetic novels based on his naval experience.

Pallas The 'Collection Pallas' was published in Paris in the years around 1914, and included Pierre Vrignault's *Anthologie de la chanson française*, as well as anthologies of English literature.

Plutarch (46?-120?) Greek philosopher and biographer, best known as author of 46 'Parallel Lives' of Greeks and Romans, which in Sir Thomas North's version (1579) was an important source for the Elizabethan playwrights.

Pierre de Ronsard (1524-1585), French poet, principal figure in the 'Pleiade', a group of seven poets in the later half of the sixteenth century.

Rural Rides See Cobbett.

Sir Walter Scott (1771-1832), poet and novelist, for whose novels Gurney had a continued enthusiasm.

Specimens See Lamb.

Spirit of Man See Bridges.

Robert Louis Stevenson (1850-1894), novelist, essayist and poet; Gurney was very enthusiastic about his letters.

Table Talk See Hazlitt.

Edward Thomas (1878-1917), poet; Gurney's friend John Haines knew him well and Gurney considered himself an 'E.T. enthusiast'

Virgil (70-19 B.C.), Roman poet; Gurney could respond to the mixture of poetry, war, wandering and return in the *Aeneid*.

Wild Wales See Borrow.

W.B. Yeats (1865-1939), Irish poet, several of whose poems were set by Gurney.

America and Americans

Gurney was interested in Alan Seeger (1888-1916), but his greatest stimulus to interest in America comes from Walt Whitman (1819-1892), whose *Leaves of Grass* Gurney rediscovered in 1915. Gurney's love of American names derive from Whitman and an atlas. See for example 'Reference Map of the Civil War' (GA 21A.96-7), where he writes that 'the map standing for Provinces outruns / My mind'. His litany of names is therefore an imaginary America. and includes Boston, Hartford, Long Island, Manhattan, Providence, Plymouth and Salem.

Stars

In October 1915, Gurney wrote to Marion Scott that 'the sight of Orion and the three stars near by moves me as much as Beethoven' (*Letters* p.51). That sense of something beyond the ordinary remains with Gurney and he refers to both familiar and unfamiliar celestial bodies; in these two books he mentions Capella, Eridanus, Jupiter, Orion, Regulus, the Pleiads, Sirius and Venus.

Index of Titles and First Lines

(For the purposes of this index, the definite and indefinite articles are ignored in titles; titles are printed in italic)